Kena Upaniṣad

Rediscovering Indian Literary Classics
(ISSN - 0972-0111)

1. Taittirīya Upaniṣad: With the Original Text in Sanskrit and Roman Transliteration; by Muni Narayana Prasad. (ISBN 978-81-246-0014-6)

2,4-5. Bṛhadāraṇyaka Upaniṣad: With Original Text in Roman Transliteration. English Translation and Appendices; by Nitya Chaitanya Yati; Vol. 1: Madhu Kāṇḍa; Vol. 2: Muni Kāṇḍa; Vol. 3: Khila Kāṇḍa. (ISBN 978-81-246-0008-5)

3. Kena Upaniṣad: With the Original Text in Sanskrit and Roman Transliteration; by Muni Narayana Prasad. (ISBN 978-81-246-0034-4)

6. Muṇḍaka Upaniṣad: With the Original Text in Sanskrit and Roman Transliteration; by Muni Narayana Prasad. (ISBN 978-81-246-0105-1)

7. Kaṭha Upaniṣad: With the Original Text in Sanskrit and Roman transliteration; by Muni Narayana Prasad. (ISBN 978-81-246-0110-5)

8. Praśna Upaniṣad: With the Original Text in Sanskrit and Roman transliteration; by Muni Narayana Prasad. (ISBN 978-81-246-0129-7)

9. Aitareya Upaniṣad: With the Original Text in Sanskrit and Roman transliteration; by Muni Narayana Prasad. (ISBN 978-81-246-0142-6)

10. Śrī Dakṣiṇāmūrti Stotram of Śrī Śaṅkarācārya; with the commentary Tattva Prakāśikā; by Swami Tattvavidananda Saraswati; Edited by Puppala B. (ISBN 978-81-246-0210-2)

11. Āditya Hṛdayam: With the Commentary Tattvaprakāśikā; by Swami Tattvavidananda Saraswati (ISBN 978-81-246-0231-7)

12. Vāstuśāstra: Ancient Indian Architecture and Civil Engineering — Retrospects and Prospects; by Rahul Kumar Altekar (ISBN 978-81-246-0246-1)

13. Gaṇapati Upaniṣad: With the Commentary Tattvaprakāśikā; by Swami Tattvavidananda Saraswati (ISBN 978-81-246-0265-2)

14. Life's Pilgrimage Through the Gītā; by Swami Muni Narayana Prasad (ISBN 978-81-246-0310-9)

15. Chāndogya Upaniṣad: With the Original Text in Sanskrit and Roman transliteration; by Swami Muni Narayana Prasad (ISBN 978-81-246-0374-1)

Rediscovering Indian Literary Classics, no. 3

Kena Upaniṣad

with the original text in Sanskrit and Roman transliteration

Translation with an
Extensive Commentary by
Swami Muni Narayana Prasad

D.K. Printworld (P) Ltd.
Publishers of Indian Traditions

Cataloging in Publication Data — DK
[Courtesy: D.K. Agencies (P) Ltd. <docinfo@dkagencies.com>]

Narayana Prasad, *Muni*, 1938-
Kena Upaniṣad : with the original text in Sanskrit and roman transliteration / translation with an extensive commentary by Swami Muni Narayana Prasad. — 2nd rev. ed.
p. cm. — (Rediscovering Indian literary classics ; no. 3)
Text of Kena Upanishad in Sanskrit (Devanagari and roman); translation, commentary and introductory matter in English.
Includes bibliographical references (p.) and index.
ISBN 13: 9788124605837

1. Upanishads. Kenopaniṣad — Commentaries. I. Upanishads. Kenopaniṣad. English & Sanskrit. II. Title. III. Series: Rediscovering Indian literary classics ; no. 3.

DDC 294.59218 22

First published in 1995
Second impression in 2004
Second revised edition, 2011
ISBN 13: 978-81-246-0583-7 ISBN 10: 81-246-0583-1

Published and printed by:
D.K. Printworld (P) Ltd.
Regd. office : *'Srikunj'*, F-52, Bali Nagar
Ramesh Nagar Metro Station
New Delhi – 110 015
Phones : (011) 2545 3975; 2546 6019; *Fax* : (011) 2546 5926
e-mail: indology@dkprintworld.com
Web: www.dkprintworld.com

Preface

THE most interesting item of the daily routine of life in the *Gurukula,* ever since I became an inmate of it, had been the early morning recitation of the selected portions of the Upaniṣads. Eventually I began to explain the meaning of them to the kids in a simple way. Finally when I decided to lead the life of a renunciate, the special direction given by my Guru, Nataraja Guru, was that my *sannyāsa*-life should be centred round the Upaniṣads and their tradition.

My main interest has always been on the philosophy of Narayana Guru who had attained final *samādhi* before I was born. My acquaintance with him was only through his highly philosophical poems as interpreted by Nataraja Guru based on the dialectical way of approach, which had been known to the ancient *ṛṣis* of India as *yoga-buddhi,* as is evident from the *Bhagavad-Gītā*. Swāmī Āryabhaṭan, one of the well-known orators in the Malayalam language on spiritual matters, once told me that Narayana Guru once asked him to give lectures expounding the Upaniṣads in his own way. The Guru gave this direction when he met Swāmī Āryabhaṭan in his younger days as a talented orator. This gave me the courage to interpret the Upaniṣads in my own way. Narayana Guru's philosophy gave me an insight into many of the puzzling passages in the Upaniṣads.

I took up the *Kaṭha Upaniṣad* for giving a free interpretation, and my intention was not of writing a publishable book. My aspiration was to delve deep into the philosophy of the Upaniṣad as I was convinced that there was no other way of doing it. It was well received by readers on serializing in the Malayalam philosophical monthly, *The Gurukulam*. Then Guru Nitya Chaitanya Yati and self together resolved to write commentaries on all the ten major Upaniṣads, the *Bṛhadāraṇyaka* and *Chāndogya* to be done by him and the rest by me. But he had already written his commentary on the *Īśa* and *Māṇḍūkya Upaniṣad*s by then. I therefore actually had to do only the remaining six. That is how this series originated.

I wrote the commentaries originally in Malayalam, my mother tongue. My interpretation of the *Kaṭha Upaniṣad* was translated to English and was serialised in the *Gurukulam Quarterly* published from the United States. When I found that it was well received, I dared to make the English version of the others too.

Excepting the *Kaṭha Upaniṣad* and the *Muṇḍaka Upaniṣad* all were originally written as a result of the collective thinking of a group of research scholars who were residing with me at the *Gurukula*. I am indebted to all of them. I made the English version of the *Kena Upaniṣad*, while I was living in Fiji, a small island country in South Pacific, where I had enough spare time to concentrate on such works.

The trustees of the Gītā Āshram in Fiji were also much helpful. Dr Peter Oppenheimer of the USA took all the trouble to go through the entire text carefully and to edit it. I am grateful to all of them. I am also thankful to M/s D.K. Printworld for including my commentaries in their series "Rediscovering Indian Literary Classics."

With prostrations at the feet of both Narayana Guru and Nataraja Guru as well as the unknown *ṛṣi*s of yore, I offer this commentary on the *Kena Upaniṣad* as a forerunner to a new tradition of freely interpreting the scriptures of India, while adhering strictly to the essence of their comprehensive yet unitive philosophical vision.

25 May 1994 **Swami Muni Narayana Prasad**

Contents

Introduction

EVERY Upaniṣad is appended to a Veda forming the last part of it. So the Upaniṣads used to be called Vedāntas, meaning the end of the Vedas. The *Kena Upaniṣad* is a part of *Talavakāra Brāhmaṇa* which comes under the *Sāma Veda*. It is called so because it begins with the word *kena*. Moreover, the main problem raised and answered in this Upaniṣad is also indicated by the word *kena* which means, "by whom?" The question raised in this Upaniṣad is "By whom are all the faculties in us willed and directed?"

In another sense also the Upaniṣads could be called Vedānta. *Veda* means knowledge and *anta*, end or conclusion. Thus Vedānta means the final conclusion of knowledge. This does not mean that it enables one to know everthing knowable. Such a knowledge is impossible, and does not give us the satisfaction we seek. But there is yet another awareness, attaining which all the desires to know further ceases. That awareness makes evident to us the meaninglessness of all the knowledge that we were trying to accumulate. That awareness of self-fulfilment is the end of our search for knowledge. In that sense it could be called Vedānta. That awareness is the theme of all the Upaniṣads, and is an experience of the non-difference of our personal existence from the totality of existence. Thus we realise the ultimate meaning of our life which is one with the life of the whole. This realisation makes our life a continuity of the flow of contentment, the ultimate aim of all philosophies and also of the Upaniṣads.

The Sanskrit word for philosophy is *darśana*. *Darśana* means a vision. It is a vision of the oneness of the ends and means of life, where there is no room for the differentiation of the knower, the object of knowledge and the act of knowing. Each Upaniṣad leads us to this vision using a specific question as an instrument. The *Kena Upaniṣad* raises the question, "What is that principle which urges our mind, vitality, word and senses, to function?"

Being faithful to the traditional convention of starting a serious study with a prayerful attitude, this Upaniṣad also begins with an invocation for peace, which is called *śānti pāṭha*:

ओं आप्यायन्तु ममाङ्गानि वाक् प्राणश्चक्षुः श्रोत्रमथो बलमिन्द्रियाणि च सर्वाणि। सर्वं ब्रह्मौपनिषदं माऽहं ब्रह्म निराकुर्यां मा मा ब्रह्म निराकरोद-निराकरणमस्त्वनिराकरणं मेऽस्तु। तदात्मनि निरते य उपनिषत्सु धर्मास्ते मयि सन्तु ते मयि सन्तु॥

ओं शान्तिः शान्तिः शान्तिः॥

auṁ āpyāyantu mamāṅgāni vāk prāṇaś cakṣuḥ śrotram atho balam indriyāṇi ca sarvāṇi । *sarvaṁ brahmaupaniṣadaṁ mā 'haṁ brahma nirākuryāṁ mā mā brahma nirākarod anirākaraṇama astu anirākaraṇama me 'stu* । *tad ātmani nirate ya upaniṣatsu dharmās te mayi santu te mayi santu* ॥

auṁ śāntiḥ śāntiḥ śāntiḥ ॥

May my limbs, speech, vital breath, eyes, ears, as also my strength and all the senses grow vigorous. All this is the Absolute (*Brahman*) referred to in the Upaniṣads. May I never negate the Absolute. May the Absolute never negate me. May there be no negating. May there be non-negating in me. Let those basic tenets enunciated in the Upaniṣads, rest in the Self. Let them be in me. Aum Peace! Peace! Peace!

One yearns to know the meaning of life when it is felt that one's own existence is losing its meaning. When one's existence is fully stabilised in oneself it is called *svasthatā* in

Sanskrit, which in common usage means, a healthy condition. The feeling of instability is called *asvasthatā*. This state could be caused by an unexpected unfavourable reaction from a beloved person. Taking away from us what has been considered the most valuable or dearest may also cause the same state. A sudden attack from other beings, including germs, rendering one helpless, may also happen to be the reason. All these are sufferings caused by other beings. Such sufferings effected by other beings are called *ādhibhautika duḥkha*s in Sanskrit.

Our expectations in life are many. We always toil to fulfil them. Sometimes something untoward happens, which makes all our efforts and expectations meaningless. But had one been able to do whatever is normal with a responsible person, without any expectation about its result, this unexpected turning of events would not have caused misery. Such sufferings are thus caused by our own expectations. These self-caused sufferings are called *ādhyātmika duḥkha*s. These can happen in different fields and levels of our life, ranging from the troubles one makes for oneself because of one's foolish fancifulness, to the internal agony one feels when one has a genuine thirst for wisdom, but finds no way to quench it.

Sometimes unexpected tragedies happen to us by the decision of Providence, as it were. At that moment we may feel as if we were thrown into the abyss of a black hole. Sometimes an entire family disappears from our midst, when met with a tragic accident. By chance an infant child of the family could be seen lying safely at a distance, innocent of all the vicissitudes of life. At that moment even the smile of the child would be taken by us as part of a pathetic scene. Such sufferings, caused not by the fault of any one, are termed *ādhidaivika duḥkha*s.

Our wish is to avoid all sufferings in life. But we know, it is not within our power to avoid them fully. By experience we learn that what others can do to help us in this respect is also little. The only remaining way is to seek the help of God. So we pray. The teachings of the Upaniṣads are meant to put an end to all the sufferings of life. Hence it is only normal to begin and end the wisdom teaching with such a prayer. The texts of all the Upaniṣads are conventionally sandwiched between such prayers which are called *śānti pāṭhas*.

One who is physically very weak due to starvation or for other reasons will not be able to concentrate on the lessons on high philosophy. Both mental and physical efforts require a healthy body. Provisions to keep our physical system in full vigorousness are already available in the overall system of nature. The discussion in this Upaniṣad is centred round the problem, in whose imagination and by whose will is all this well arranged. The present Peace Invocation begins with a prayer for the vigour of our physical system as well as of the senses. It admits also that all this is only an external manifestation of the one Reality or *Brahman*. It is this Reality, as visualised by a *ṛṣi* (seer), that is wrapped up in words and presented to us in the form of Upaniṣads. Our attempt then is to unwrap it and to see for ourselves what is inside. Making this vision our own is not possible with the aid of any external means or through logical reasoning. What we have to do is only not to deny that Reality that is already here in the form of "I," the seeker. On not denying the Reality already in us, which is not something else to be known or attained, we are already in the experience of oneness with that Reality. This experience of oneness is sometimes called *sāyujya*.

This non-denial of the Reality by us, and the non-denial of us by the Reality, is what is prayed for in this Peace Invocation. As this non-denial becomes real, one feels that one and the same Reality functions as the all-sustaining principle. A sustaining principle is called *dharma*. Finally, we see that it is this *dharma* that is hidden in the Upaniṣads, wrapped up by their words.

This visualisation takes us beyond the level of our personal interests and personal sufferings. We feel always, even in our routine works, at one with the Total. Then, what we do in everyday life is only our conscious participation with the creativity of the Total. What happens to each of us every moment is only part of the total system of life. The individual, as the doer and the enjoyer, then gains a kind of neutral attitude towards his or her own personal joys and sufferings. This is the only way we can free ourselves of the sufferings of life and be peaceful.

The repetition of the word "Peace!" three times at the end indicates our aspiration for freedom from the three kinds of sufferings and the resultant attainment of peace.

1

Section One

केनेषितं पतति प्रेषितं मनः
केन प्राणः प्रथमः प्रैति युक्तः।
केनेषितां वाचमिमां वदन्ति
चक्षुः श्रोत्रं क उ देवो युनक्ति ॥ १ ॥

keneṣitam patati preṣitaṁ manaḥ
kena prāṇaḥ prathamaḥ praiti yuktaḥ ।
keneṣitām vācam imāṁ vadanti
cakṣuḥ śrotram ka u devo yunakti ॥ 1 ॥

Willed by whom does the mind fall on its objects? Conjoined by whom does the vital breath move, as it were the first? At whose will do people utter this speech? Which god is it that urges the eyes and ears on?

On opening today's newspaper I read the sad news of injustice done to the black people of South Africa, merely because they were black. I sat down for a moment thinking of social prejudices and their tragic consequences, which exist only due to the ignorance of man. My mood changed after a while. I began to think, "Why should I be bothered about all this? It doesn't affect me. It is not my problem."

Thus we can grow in our mind to embrace the entire human race, and also we can shrink ourselves to the shell of our personal interests. Both happen in our minds. We feel we are soaring up in our minds when we identify ourselves with the total. And when we shrink ourselves to our personal interests, we feel we are falling down. This going up and down depends upon our interests. We might also find ourselves facing the danger of neglecting our own personal matters, when we deliberately try to be broad-minded. After a while our mind pulls us back to ourselves. It might so happen also that when we live caring for our own affairs, our neighbours are put to troubles simply because of our neglect. This makes us feel remorse and compels us to care for others too. That means, our attempt to bring our minds under our full control also creates problems very often.

Do I control my mind, or does my mind control me? Or, is there a third factor that controls me and my mind?

I see an expansive world before me. It is infinite. But do my eyes reach the infinite expansiveness and directly perceive it? No. My visual field is only a tiny portion of the visible world. I add to this portion of the world directly seen, the unseen expansiveness and comprehend all together as "the visible world." I don't have even the slightest doubt about the existence of the unseen part of the "visible" world, even though I visualise it only in my mind. It is the hope of seeing things directly if we go where they are, that compels us to believe in their existence.

In fact, a lion's share of what we call the visible world exists only in our imagination. Even the pen with which I am writing these lines is not fully visible to me. When I see its one side the other side remains invisible. As I turn it around and see the other side, the former becomes invisible. Yet I take for granted that I am seeing the pen in its complete shape. Actually the fullness of its shape is only in my imagination.

The form of the world that is in my imagination may contain in it the memories of past experiences and also the fancied forms of all that will possibly be seen in future. In both cases, our minds have a decisive role in giving shape to that world.

Memory and its Physical Basis

Let us take the case of what I see directly in the visual field. I do not recognise what I see just by seeing it. When I see an object, I correlate it with the memories of my past experiences and recognise each item as such and such a thing. There is no possibility of recognising things in the absence of these memories. That means, the role of our minds even in our direct perception is a major one. In short, our minds play a significant role in conceiving a perceptual world which consists of both the seen and the unseen.

This correlation of imagination and direct vision in our perceptual knowledge does not happen as controlled by me. The process of adding what is in imagination to the actual sense perception is called brain perception in modern psychology. Who envisaged such a perceptual experience?

Modern science also claims to know how memories are stored up in our brain. It has been discovered that certain changes happening at the synapse of neurons in the area called hippocampus is the physical basis for storing up memories. A rushing of calcium particles from the pre-synaptic axon terminal to the post-synaptic axon terminal happens when an electrical impulse is transmitted from the former to the latter. These calcium particles activate the enzyme called calpain. This renders fodrin or the outer wall of the neuron very weak. The repetition of this process causes some new growth at the synapses or some alteration in the already existing growths, and these get stabilised. The latest assumption of modern science is that these growths or alterations at the synapses are the physical bases of stored-up memories. But no claim is made that this is a final conclusion. The complexity and diversity of the process of memorising are so vast that our attempt to explain that process results in over-simplifying it. We know for sure that what we experience as a memory is not just a nodule at the synapses of a neuron-transmitter.

It was not I who correlated my experience called memory with the physical changes in the neurons. It does not happen under my control. But it is certain that there will be no memory in the absence of such a correlation. It is this faculty of memory that enables man to acquire any knowledge and to travel even through the expansiveness of the empty space. Who has correlated this noble faculty of memory, which has been the basis for all the achievements of mankind, with the physical appearance of a nodule at the terminal of a neuron?

My Physical Existence is Unbounded

I know, my physical existence is bounded by the outer skin of my body and what keeps this physical body alive is the process of respiration. The inhalation and exhalation can be normalised to a certain extent by turning our attention to the breathing process. But it cannot be controlled as I like. In the normal course it is an involuntary function of our physical system. It is the air that surrounds me that sustains me through the breathing process without the gap of even a minute.

In other words, the air that surrounds me is a vital part of my physical existence. And the air that surrounds me extends to the atmosphere that envelops the earth. Wherever I go around the earth, the air in the atmosphere of that locality becomes the air to be inhaled by me. Now I find that my physical existence extends as far as the atmosphere goes. The same air goes into the minutest cell of my body and imparts the vitality to be alive. I have no control over this system that brings into one fold the existence of a minute cell in a living body and the entire atmosphere surrounding the earth. It is the function of breath that brings together these two extremely opposite poles, one representing the microcosm and the other the macrocosm. Who did bring these together into one functional system by which life became possible?

The Internal and the External

Everything is understood as pertaining to the objective or subjective world. They are real in the form we experience. This experience could either be of the external world or of the internal world. But experience as such cannot be either external or internal. These two have a mutually complementary role in giving integrity and unity to all our experiences. Experience, as an awareness pure and simple, is unconditioned and absolute, while the externality or internality of the factors that make it specific, are conditioning factors. These render the awareness relative. Thus our experience of the world and visualisation of ourselves together make a systematized whole, a blend of relative and non-relative experiences. Experiences are mysteriously multifarious. The contentment of life depends on how far we see this mysterious multifariousness of existence as our own self-content.

The Second Self of Man

Man is not satisfied merely by experiencing this contentment. He also wants to recreate it and to find self-contentment in that creativeness. This may be considered as one of the most sublime aspects of human life. We use different media for this re-creation of one's self-experience. Word is the most popular among them. It is the union of mind and word that gives a living content to languages. This union creates a world of its own.

The *Bṛhadāraṇyaka Upaniṣad*[1] gives the status of a second self of man to the world of words created thus. There is no field of human life that cannot be made the meaning content of words. It is words that help us in our daily transactions of life. The same word could also convey the overwhelming mystical experiences of seers. This latter one could be considered the ultimate limit of the capability of words to contain a meaning. At this limiting point the word is often equated to the ultimate Reality and is called *śabda-brahman* by Indians.

Word and its Role in Life

When we hear uttered words or read written sentences, it is not the uttered sounds or the funny black lines on a sheet of paper that come to our attention. What we grasp is the meaning content the sounds or scribblings contain in themselves as words. Mere sounds or lines are transformed here into symbols which could meaningfully convey the most sublime mystical experiences as well as the affairs of mundane transactions.

How did these symbols, which we call words, gain the power to re-create the expansiveness of our experiences? Man is part of this universe. He re-creates a universe by himself with the help of words. This newly created universe has the advantage of being transmittable to another individual, where words play the role of a medium. This communicability of feelings and experiences through words and other similar media integrates the entire human race into one family. Words serve here as a golden thread that strings together the entire human race.

For the same reason a word of a wise man is enough to save the entire race from total destruction. By the same token,

---

1. *Bṛhadāraṇyaka Upaniṣad*, I.ii.4.

a word of an indiscriminate egotist could cause the annihilation of the human race.

Thus the power of words is immense and endless. It has a crucial role to play in the meaningfulness of human life. Whose intentionality played in such a programming of life?

Sense-Perception

The ability to formulate ideas and to weave out mental imageries is natural with us, and this faculty is what enables us to re-create a universe of our own, using words. Memory of our past experiences plays a major role in formulating ideas and imageries.

It is through our sense organs we get the primary experiences. Sense-perception happens when our sense organs come into contact with their respective objects.

How does it happen? Is it a process in which something external is reflected in the mind, just like a mirror image? Or, does consciousness go out and assume the form of the object?

Modern biology and psychology give us an explanation of the process of sense-perception. According to them, when something is seen, the sunlight that is reflected by the object crosses the lenses of our eyes and falls on the retina where it causes some electrical stimulations to the nerve-endings of the central nervous systems. These electrical impulses are conveyed to the brain through a transmitting and receiving system in neurons. Finally when they reach the visual area of the brain, they cause certain biochemical changes in its structure. It is these changes we experience as perceptual knowledge. But neither biology nor psychology enlightens us on how certain biochemical changes, mere physical events, are transformed into experiences in the form of pleasures and pains, ideas and imageries, which sometimes find expression as poems, paintings, stories or just a smile.

But the philosophers of India give us a different picture of the process of sense-perception. Their explanation is based on the acceptance of one basic Reality existing in and as everything. That one Reality appears as many. The substance of that Reality is Consciousness (*cit*). In other words, one and the same indivisible Consciousness appears on the one side as the knower and as the known on the other. In the process of perception, the Consciousness that is already conditioned and delimited as the knower, finds a way out through the vents of sense organs and reaches the objects, and identifies with the form of the objects. What is called object is also another conditioned state of Consciousness-Reality. Sense-perception is a process by which two conditioned aspects of the one unconditioned Consciousness meet together and merge in the neutrality of the same Consciousness. It is the way the one homogeneous content of Consciousness in both the knower and known is realized.

Visual perception admittedly occurs only when there is light outside, and when the reflected light enters the pupils of our eyes. But we find also that day-dreamers do not see anything around though they are awake and the entrances for the external stimulations remain open. A person in coma does not perceive anything, though his internal functions are going on normally and all the sense organs are open to be stimulated from outside. In the case of day-dreamers, it is the absence of interest that blocks the way to sense impression, while it is the absence of the illumination from within that disables the man in coma to perceive. Sense-perception, thus, is a confection of the stimulation of the senses from external objects, the interest to receive the stimulations, and the conscious illumination from inside which awakens our interests and enlivens the senses. The concept that the object known is external and the knower is internal is then the result of the conditioning with which our mind functions.

In no way we can causally relate the physical events that happen in the bodily system and the awareness called perception either. The objects, sense organs, neural system and the chemical changes in it, consciousness — all these really are various factors involved in the context of the event of sense-perception. One need not be the cause of another. But the interaction of these factors actualises the event of sense perception, the basis for our world vision. Whose conscious direction did plan all these delicate arrangements?

Such is the major problem raised in this Upaniṣad. As already mentioned, all these questions and the similar ones could be summarized into one word, *kena* (by whom).

If we say, in scientific jargon, that the entire system consisting of the internal and external factors and faculties functions as if in a computer programme, who was the programmer of this programming?

Though all the Upaniṣads generally are dialogues between *guru*s and disciples, the smaller Upaniṣads do not mention who the *guru* is and who the disciple is. In some cases, as in the *Īśa Upaniṣad* and the *Māṇḍūkya Upaniṣad,* no question is even asked. In the case of the present Upaniṣad, the question is given, but the *guru* and disciple are not named. We have to see ourselves as the questioners.

श्रोत्रस्य श्रोत्रं मनसो मनो यद्
वाचो ह वाचं स उ प्राणस्य प्राणः ।
चक्षुषश्चक्षुरतिमुच्य धीराः
प्रेत्यास्माल्लोकादमृता भवन्ति ॥ २ ॥

śrotrasya śrotraṁ manaso mano yad
vāco ha vācaṁ sa u prāṇasya prāṇaḥ ।
cakṣuṣaś cakṣur atimucya dhīrāḥ
pretyāsmāl lokād amṛtā bhavanti ॥ 2 ॥

For the reason that it indeed is the Ear of the ear, the Mind of the mind, the Speech of the speech, the Breath of the breath, the Eye of the eye, the wise ones, on becoming Liberated and going forward from this world, become immortal.

Any enquiry, by necessity, has to begin from the realm of what is directly known, and proceed to what is yet to be known. We possess ears, mind, the ability to communicate, sense organs and so on as means of knowing. The enquiry in this Upaniṣad is centred round the problem, who did all this programming in which every functional faculty in us is delicately but invariably made related to an external element, in such a way that each of them has a place in our experience of the world.

The Human Bio-computer

The function of our brain is very often compared to the working of a computer. A computer is able to think for us. It keeps in it whatever we want to keep in our memory, and it provides us with the required information as and when required. It can even correct our mistakes. But the creation of such a thinking machine requires another intelligence which foresees the entire structure of it and how each part of it fulfils its role in ensuring the net result. That intelligence should see in advance what kind of mechanical arrangements a computer should have, what kind of mechanical changes will result when power passes through it, how the flow of power and the mechanical arrangements are to be organised in such a way as to give the required result, what kind of data should be recorded in the software to enable it to react as we want, and numerous other details.

When the computer works properly we do not see the programmer who worked behind it. It is not even possible to find him out with the help of the computer. We appreciate the intelligence who devised it, when we see that the machine shows the signs of human intelligence. Sometimes we even feel wonderstruck.

The human brain is like a very complicated computer. The difference is that it is a bio-computer. If we were to make a mechanical computer to replace a human brain, it would need a space kilometres across to accommodate it. The human bio-computer has some more notable peculiarities. While the mechanical computer reacts according to a programme already fed into it, the human bio-computer's function is decided by the objects external to it also, the interest one has in the particular object, and the conscious inflaming that sets our cognitive, volitional and creative faculties to function, stimulated by the interest we have on the object. In other words, the human bio-computer is constituted not only of the grey material called brain. All the factors mentioned above form essential parts of it.

Computer and Intuition

As in the case of the ordinary computer, the programmer remains invisible in the case of the human biocomputer also, and cannot be found out utilising the searching capability of it. In one sense, we can say that the computer's search is a logically forward movement, while the search for its programmer has to be, by necessity, a reverse one. This kind of looking backward logically, is what is called intuitive search. In Sanskrit this way of searching is called *antarmukha anveṣaṇa* (inward search). A general inclination of mind towards this kind of thinking, is called introvertedness in psychology.

The ability of ears to hear a sound is a kind of forward movement, while he who enables the ears to hear has to be looked for backwards or rather inwards. The reasoning of our mind is always about something which our mind tries to grasp as if through a forward movement. But to think about that which makes the mind move forward, we have again to look backwards or inwards. The reference to the Ear of the ear, the Mind of the mind, the Speech of the speech, etc. in the Upaniṣad indicates the necessity of such a reversal of the order of thinking in our search for a final answer to the question raised here.

The Programmer

The computer was computed or mathematically visualised by a human consciousness. Similarly, it must be a consciousness that heard the ear and thought of the mind. That which spoke of the speech, saw the eyes, and breathed the breath, was also a consciousness.

Are all these one consciousness or different consciousnesses? What we call hearing, seeing, thinking, etc. are only different functional modulations of one consciousness. There is no room, therefore, for more than one consciousness behind these functions. Methodologically, our inwardly or negatively turned enquiry, which starts from many facets, leads us to the reality of one consciousness which always remains as the original source of everything. Ontologically speaking, what we have to deal with in our transactions is a world of multiplicity, but the ultimate Reality that exists in and through all these ever-changing phenomenal appearances is only one.

The Reality that underlies the phenomenal modulations of my consciousness underlies not only mine. It is the same consciousness that underlies in others and in the infinite appearances that constitute the visible world, of which I am a part. It sees not only my eyes, it is the eye of the entire system of life too. While it hears my ears, it hears the entire system of life too, and so on. That Reality is pure Consciousness or *cit* in essence. It is not my consciousness or of someone else. It is just awareness pure and simple. Because there is nothing outside its bounds, it is also called *Brahman*, the English equivalent to which is "the Absolute." The ontological existence of myself and of that Reality as awareness are not two but one. When this unity becomes a living experience, all the feverishness of life becomes cooled down.

Fear and its Removal

Fear is the one emotion which reigns supreme in the usual course of our life. We are afraid of those around us; we are afraid of wild animals; we are afraid of God and also of Nature. Our belief in the unknown ghosts and spirits becomes dreadful to us. The topmost fear is that of death.

Though fear is common among all living beings, man is the only being who plans his life seeing in advance all the possible dangers. In all the other animals we see only an instinctive effort for self-preservation and to avoid dangers. Man, only because of fear, likes to live under the protection of arms and sometimes with bodyguards. To save himself from animals and nature, man makes secure quarters. Afraid of the changes in the weather conditions, he likes to have air-conditioned living quarters, if possible. He makes temples or other centres of worship, because he is afraid of God. He also makes offerings to gods as a measure to safeguard himself from their wraths. Even imprecatory rituals are performed in order to save himself from the fear of ghosts and spirits. Medicines and even magical spells are relied on to safeguard us from diseases and death. Man will not hesitate to do anything to save himself from death. He will be willing even to give up everything for that.

It is only natural that our future generation will also have ability to work and live by themselves as we do. But there is an instinctive fear that they might not be able to live by themselves. Parents even wish their descendants to live without doing anything, as doing work itself turns out to be dangerous. So they hoard wealth. As a result, they have to live a life of incessant insecurity.

Our efforts to find security from fear thus puts us to further dangers. In short, freedom from fear, including that of death, is the only panacea to make life really an incessant flow of contentment.

What is it that I am afraid of? It should be something other than me. There is only one entity that I am not afraid of. It is myself. (The nervous tension resulted by fear sometimes turns out to be a pathological condition of fearing oneself. That is only a case of exception.)

We have already seen that what we call "I" is not just the vital breath or mind or the sense organs, but it is the consciousness that is behind all these. What underlies behind all the manifested aspects is called *sat* in Sanskrit, which means, Existence. The content of this existence is Consciousness. The Sanskrit term for consciousness is *cit*. So the real "I" is often referred to as *sat* and *cit* at the same time. The realisation that the real content of myself is the existent Consciousness, also reveals the reality that it is the Reality behind everything. In other words, the real content of myself and of what is called others is one only. Finally we become convinced that there is nothing that can be called "the other."

When there is no "other" existing, there is nothing to be afraid of. This state of absolute fearlessness is called *abhayam* in Sanskrit. So the *Bṛhadāraṇyaka Upaniṣad* defines *Brahman* or the Absolute as this state of fearlessness or *abhayam*.[2] There are many references in other Upaniṣads also in which the ultimate Reality or *Brahman* is equated to *abhayam*. This state is the final self-contentment or bliss (*ānanda*) aspired for by seekers. This *ānanda* is also experienced in Consciousness which is Existent. That is the reason why traditionally the ultimate Reality is often defined as *sat-cit-ānanda* (Existence-Consciousness-value-sense).

Śaṅkara, in his *Vivekacūḍāmaṇi*, insists that what a *guru* has to offer first of all to a restless seeker is *abhayam*.[3] One who has found one's secure and fearless abode in the ultimate Reality, has already crossed over from the world of death to the world of immortality. The ultimate Reality, the Substance that abides in my being also, is birthless and deathless. I am also therefore birthless and deathless.

One who has such an understanding is called *dhīra* (a wise one). He knows that what we experience as pleasures and pains are merely momentary spurtings of the immortal value-sense of the Self. One who knows this, and sticks to this wisdom, and imparts the same wisdom to others, is to be called a *dhīra*, according to the etymological derivation of this word. This knowledge cannot be imparted to others through a course of instruction. When someone, who is restless because of the fear of the mundane world, comes across a person who is the embodiment of fearlessness, he or she finds a secure abode in that person.

The word *pretya* is often translated as "after death." According to Vedānta, life has to be a progression from the world of death to deathlessness or immortality. One who

2. *abhayam vai brahma*, ibid., IV.iv.25.

3. *Vivekacūḍāmaṇi* — verse 43.

has realised one's Reality as the immortal Self, has already freed oneself from the world of death. He will not be concerned with the state of affairs after death. In what we call life, death and the state after death, he sees only the incessant appearance and disappearance of the manifestations of the one Reality which is *sat, cit* and *ānanda*.

न तत्र चक्षुर् गच्छति न वाग् गच्छति नो मनः ।
न विद्मो न विजानीमो यथैतदनुशिष्यात् ॥ ३ ॥

na tatra cakṣur gacchati na vāg gacchati no manaḥ ।
na vidmo na vijānīmo yathaitad anuśiṣyāt ॥ 3 ॥

अन्यदेव तद् विदितादथो अविदितादधि ।
इति शुश्रुम पूर्वेषां ये नस्तद् व्याचचक्षिरे ॥ ४ ॥

anyad eva tad viditād atho aviditād adhi ।
iti śuśruma pūrveṣāṁ ye nas tad vyācacakṣire ॥ 4 ॥

There the eye goes not, speech goes not, nor the mind. We know not That. We know not either how It could be taught. Other, indeed, is It than the known, and also It is above the unknown. Thus we have heard from the ancient ones who have explained It to us.

We have seen the process of sense-perception. In the case of seeing, it can be understood as a process in which consciousness goes out through the outlet of eyes and becomes identified with the form of the object. This is the version of Indian philosophers, while the scientists hold that it is a process of external light falling in the eyes and causing certain biochemical changes in the visual area of the brain. In both cases it is essential that there should be a contact of a sense organ with an object. But the eye or any other sense organ does not have any such contact with the Eye of the eye, or the Ear of the ear, mentioned in the previous *mantra*.

That ultimate Reality is thus not visible to eyes or any other sense. We know, we have to find out that Reality, because that is the only eternal meaning of our life. But we are as if at a loss as our senses are not capable of grasping it. These senses are all oriented towards external objects. This ultimate Reality, as we have seen, is to be found out by turning our attention inwards. The *Kaṭha Upaniṣad* allegorically states that the self-created Creator created human beings with all their senses turned outwards as if it was a punishment.[4]

We could say that the process of sense-perception is a linear one. The experience we gain by it takes us forward from one object to another. It is the same with our reasoning power also. But in the case of the search for the Reality which is the Eye of the eye, instead of going forward in a linear way, the enquiry should turn back to itself the enquirer turns back to himself. The linear nature of sense-perception is indicated by the words, "there the eye goes not." In Narayana Guru's words, the search for the Reality is a knowledge that is even above knowledge.[5]

How is a Word Formulated?

The *ṛṣis* of India, who were also psychologists, saw the process of expressing an idea as having four stages. They are called *parā* (the transcendent), *paśyanti* (visualisation), *madhyamā* (medium), and *vaikharī* (the uttered word). The causal Reality, Consciousness in essence, is *parā* or the transcendent. Without it nothing happens. In that Consciousness happens the formulation of an idea or experience that has a specific form. The visualisation of that form is called *paśyanti*. This vision has to be brought into the mould of a medium in order to express it. This medium could be a language, mere sound

4. *Kaṭha Upaniṣad*, II.i.1.
5. Cf. *Ātmopadeśa Śatakam* (One Hundred Verses of Self-Instruction) verse 1.

(music), colour, or even concrete forms as in sculptures. This is the third stage called *madhyamā* or medium. The last stage is the expressed form of it, either as words or music, or any other form of expression. This stage is called *vaikharī* which means the uttered word. The word, the commenest way of communicating ideas, stands here for all the forms of expression.

What a word can do is to express an idea or an experience, that belongs to the second stage of *paśyanti*. Word cannot contain the transcendent as its meaning. It is that transcendent that made the specific vision find expression through words.

What is Mind?

And what is mind? How does it function? *Manas* is the Sanskrit word for mind. But the word *manas* has a specific meaning while the English word "mind" is much broader. The questioning, doubting and imagining faculty of our psyche is called *manas* by Indian psychologists. But there should be some primary prompting force which directs us to question, to doubt and to imagine.

The Indian seers see desire as this prompting force. The *R̥g Veda* says:

> Desire (*kāma*) was the original development (of the one) which was the first sowing (*retas*) of *manas*.[6]

The same is found repeated in the *Atharva Veda*.[7] It is usually conceived that desire happens in the mind. But what we call mind or *manas* is a function of consciousness instigated by desire. Really what we call mind is not an entity. It is only a function. The notion of *libido* in the Western psychology

6. *R̥g Veda*, X.129.4.
7. *Atharva Veda*, XIX.52.

may be considered as the modern equivalent to this *manas*. The desire that takes place in consciousness urges itself for its fulfilment. The resultant internal function is called *manas*.

This desire could be diverse in nature. At the one extreme, it could be the desire to find out the content of one's own existence. At the other extreme it could be the desire to eternalise oneself through progeny, which manifests itself as sexual urge. Such an effort of consciousness urged by a particular desire is called *manas*. When that urge is of the former kind, the same mind transforms itself to be the *sādhanā* or self-regulated discipline for the final attainment, acceptable to Vedānta. Mind, thus, becoming the object of its own search, with itself as a means, is a cyclic function that comes back to itself.

All the other mental functions are linear in nature as in the case of sense-perception. They lead us from one item of interest to another. Such a linear process never leads us to our ultimate aim, i.e., to find out the Mind that desired the mind to function.

A thirst for knowledge is the main distinguishing characteristic of man. The ultimate knowledge is an end in itself. It is not meant for gaining anything else. Self-satisfaction is the only goal of knowledge. There are knowledges which we gain not for their own sake, but to ensure some other goal, such as professional skills. Such skills cannot be considered knowledge in its strict sense. To avoid this confusion, knowledge for its own sake is called wisdom. The only goal of wisdom is self-contentment or *ānanda*. Thus, what we called *kāma*, the primeval seed of mind, and *ānanda* are not different.

Our yearning for wisdom is helped by our faculties called *karaṇas*. Sense organs, internal faculties called *manas, buddhi, citta* and *ahaṁkāra* (mind, intellect, relational mind, and I-sense), and organs of action constitute the *karaṇas*, which literally means, instruments. Among those instruments, the internal faculties are very often bracketed together and called mind or *manas*. All these instruments are, as we have seen, prompted to action by an inherent urge of the Self to realise happiness or *ānanda*, which in reality is its own self-content, or our own self-content.

The Unknowability of Reality

Consciousness has its own mode of functioning to acquire knowledge. This functional system has senses and mental faculties as its instruments. Senses get into contact with what is to be observed, and what is observed is ascertained by the reasoning faculty (*buddhi*) with the help of our previous experiences stored up in our memory (*citta*). How does this newly known object affect oneself is assessed by *ahaṁkāra* or I-sense. Thus a new item of knowledge is made part of our experience. This is the mode of operation of our acquiring knowledge. Our knowledge of this system is made precise and faultless with the help of science.

Modern science, especially physics, has played an important role in extending our range of vision both microscopically and macroscopically. At both these extremes science is facing a paradoxical situation. At the microscopic level, the subatomic particle has been found to be the basic physical reality. But its nature is so elusive that it appears to be a thing (particle) and no-thing (wave) alternately, just because it is being observed. That means, its real nature can never be determined, as its nature changes when observed. So physicists had to accept indeterminism to define what is basically real.

In the macrocosmic level, the big bang theory has become

the most acceptable concept to explain the origin of the universe. According to this theory, the universe came out of a big explosion called the big bang. What was the thing that exploded? Our scientists have decided that this question need not be asked. Time also began with this explosion. So we cannot ask, what was "before" the explosion, because there is no "before" and "after" where there is no time! According to the big bang theory, time's arrow is now moving forward and the universe is expanding. But there should be an end to the process of expansion, which started with the big-bang, and after that the time should move backwards and the universe should contract. This process should naturally end in a big-crunch. What will be there after the big-crunch? The question has no relevance as there will be no time "after" the big-crunch!

All these undefinable and illogical concepts have become acceptable to science. Such is the case when we confine our enquiry to the realm of the physical world. There is no wonder then that the Reality that remains as the Eye of the eye, the Ear of the ear, and the Mind of the mind, cannot be known by the usual way of knowing. It is the fundamental Reality behind both the physical and the mental phenomena, and both the external and the internal. As we reach such an impasse in our enquiry, we say to ourselves, "We do not know it" or "We cannot know it" (*na vidmaḥ*). It does not mean that the Reality is unrealisable in any way. Were it so, this Upaniṣad itself would become meaningless.

How to Attain Knowledge

Along with the aspiration for knowledge, man is also endowed with a longing for imparting to others what one knows. We have seen how the ability to re-create what one knows through the union of mind and words forms the second self of man. When we aspire to know something, we naturally try to get the help of someone who knows or of some book. Our numerous educational institutions, research institutions and libraries are only an extension of this natural human urge. In spite of all these elaborate facilities, man feels unsatisfied, and he tries to attain knowledge from outstanding individuals.

The process of acquiring knowledge has two aspects. One is self-study, called *svādhyāya* in Sanskrit. The second is the instruction given by a teacher by way of explanation. This is called *pravacana*. Neither of these has necessarily to be formal. An infant, when sucking the breasts of the mother, is getting nourishment as well as the first lessons of intimacy and love. This may be considered the beginning of one's self-study. The final stage of self-study or *svādhyāya* is the contemplative self-discipline one goes through, with the intuitive vision of the non-dual Self as its goal.

A growing child would be incessantly asking, "What is this?," "How is this?," "Why is this?," and so on. Some parents find it a nuisance and discourage their children by ordering them to keep quiet. They would not have done so had it been known that the questions were part of the child's self-study. Familiarising with the first alphabets, reading words from the combination of letters, trying to broaden one's understanding by reading books, reading scriptures and trying to bring out the hidden meanings in them, are all different stages of *svādhyāya*.

Similarly, instruction also has different stages. The first instructions are from the mother herself, not through words but through silent love and fondling. In fact, the future of the child to a certain extent depends upon this silent *pravacana* or instruction given by the mother at a stage when the mind of the child has not yet acquired a form of its own. Here the instruction given by a mother could be treated as prophesying the future of the child. The word *pravacana* is used in the sense of prophecy also. Formal instruction begins with initiation of the child into the first letters. This initiation is called *vidyārambha* in India, meaning, the beginning of education. The last stage of this kind of instruction could be the final wordless teaching a *guru* imparts to a disciple, when words become silent because no word can contain the meaning intended to be conveyed. Thus, instruction ends finally in non-instruction.

Excepting the final stage where self-study turns out to be non-study, and instruction turns out to be non-instruction, all the means we have devised for conveying knowledge has some end in view. But does this means help us in knowing the conscious impetus which puts us on the search for the final goal, and adopts a means conforming to it? The means we rely on is words or speech. Does speech help us in understanding the inner mystery that remains as the Speech of speech? The answer is, "No."

How do the Words of the Upaniṣad Help Us

A doubt arises naturally: if words are incapable of imparting wisdom, then what is the use of the Upaniṣad at all? It is true, the words or their meanings will not give us the final vision of the ultimate Reality. In a way we can say that the role of the words of an Upaniṣad is that of the signs we see along highways. Just by seeing the sign, "Chennai 105 km" we do not reach Chennai. We have to travel through the road 105 km more to reach there. The sign is only to help us reach there, without missing the road. In the same way, our scriptures help us only in showing us the right path and also to remind us of the possible traps on the way to the final goal. We attain the goal only if we proceed along the path. We reach nowhere just by reading the sign and understanding its meaning. The journey has to be accomplished by ourselves. We can also say that the meaning intended to be conveyed by an Upaniṣad is securely packaged in its words and presented to us, instead of being revealed by them. So the words, "We do not know how it could be taught" are not only very meaningful, but very sweet to ruminate upon also.

In short, that which is the Ear of the ear, the Eye of the eye, and the Mind of the mind, is something beyond everything that is known. Should we then give up our present enquiry? No. There are certain rare individuals who have not only directly visualised that Reality, but have realised also that it is that Reality that appears here as ourselves.

They say, "It is even above the unknown." Really it is incomprehensible to say that something is other than everything known and at the same time above what is unknown. It indicates that we should not depend upon our reasoning alone to attain the wisdom aimed at here.

We have also to accept the words of the ones who have experienced Reality as the Substance in their own being. Such a faithful acceptance of the words of the seers and *gurus* is called *śraddhā*. *Śraddhā* has a vital role in the attainment of wisdom. In fact, our own intelligence and belief in the words of the wise ones have to go hand in hand, supporting each other, in the process of the present enquiry.

Sub-atomic particles, the basic reality of matter according to modern physics, have not been seen by anyone either with the naked eye or with the help of the most powerful microscopes. Their trajectories in the electron accelerators alone have been detected with the help of electron microscopes. But we cannot deny their existence just because they are invisible, for it is their existence that makes the existence of everything visible possible. Thus, in science we accept the existence of energy particles as a reality though indirectly. The energy particle is accepted then not as something invisible, but as a reality that is even above the realm of invisibility, because it is so undeniably real. That means, even in physics the notion that reality is beyond the realms of both the visible and the invisible, is acceptable. Let us broaden the realm of visibilty to that of knowability. Then we see that one consciousness is transformed into different items of knowledge, and that that consciousness is not knowable as an item of knowledge. Thus it is beyond knowledge. Yet it is so real that our own conscious existence becomes meaningless without it. So it is above the realm of the unknown also. The awareness a seeker gains through the contemplative process, helped by both belief and reasoning, is something immediate, i.e., with no mediation between the knower and the known.

यद् वाचानभ्युदितं येन वागभ्युद्यते ।
तदेव ब्रह्म त्वं विद्धि नेदं यदिदमुपासते ॥ ५ ॥

yad vācānabhyuditaṁ yena vāg abhyudyate ।
tad eva brahma tvaṁ viddhi nedaṁ yad idam upāsate ॥ 5 ॥

That which is not expressed through speech, but that by which speech is expressed, that verily, know thou, is *Brahman*; not what here is adored as "this."

The Mystery of the Word

Word is a mystery. It is as mysterious as the universe. The alphabet of a language consists of vowels and consonants. Consonants cannot form words without imbibing the life-giving spirit of vowels. A syllable, which is the union of a consonant and a vowel, is called *varṇa* in Sanskrit. *Varṇa* literally means, colour. A consonant by itself has no function or colouration of its own. When united with a vowel, it gains a colouration. Thus it becomes a *varṇa*.

A word is the combination of such *varṇa*s. But a word is not just the sum total of syllables. The syllables become insignificant in a word as the idea enfolded by them becomes significant. A set of syllables which does not signify any such meaning does not form a word.

A word explodes into a meaning in the mind, which process is called *sphoṭa* in Sanskrit. We are capable of interlacing such meanings in our experience and create a world of words.

Narayana Guru, in one context, visualises this world as constituted of three factors. The first consists of countless words and the second of the countless ideas interlaced in our mind, and the third consists of the countless corresponding objects which could be something that exists externally and internally in the form of mental imageries.[8]

What a word can do is to contain an idea. Ideas never exist singly. They are always interlaced. The more the complexity of intermingling and integrity of ideas, the less becomes the ability of words to comprehend or convey them. Words are totally at a loss when the meaning to be conveyed attains the dimension of the all-inclusive one Reality.

The one Reality that remains unperceivable and yet undeniable, even after everything that is perceivable is perceived, is the observing consciousness. This observing consciousness is what we call "I." We are under the illusion that the observing consciousness is very limited in extent. But on closely examining we find that its extensiveness is

8. *Advaita Dīpikā*, verse 1.

limitless as nothing is outside its purview. In the sense that it is limitless in extent it is also called *Brahman*. The word *Brahman* is derived from the root *bṛh* which means, to grow limitlessly. As the all-pervading Reality, it is also called *Ātman* (the Self).

Upāsanā

Brahman is the absolute Reality, which is the Mind of the mind and the Eye of the eye. It is Consciousness pure and simple. No word can contain it as its meaning. It is in this Consciousness that words, their meanings and all the ideas find their apparent existence. Because this Consciousness itself is the essence of our own (the observer's) being, our love for the same also attains absolute dimension.

The emotion we feel towards whatever is dear is love. The Self is the dearest of all the loveables. In the usual course of life, love is always towards something other than ourselves. Love becomes all the more actual when the beloved entity has a concrete form. We like to be near that beloved one, and if possible to do service to it or him or her. Being near the beloved and doing service to it together is called *upāsanā* in Sanskrit. It is also the word for doing worship and adoration. Here the beloved is *Brahman* or the Absolute which we experience as our own self-existence. We cannot love the Self as an object, and go near and do service to it. It is not something we can refer to as "this" or "that."

An Analysis of the Self

Narayana Guru makes an original and revealing analysis of the function of consciousness from this point of view. The Consciousness which is one and unconditioned, has infinite potentials inherent in it. These powers are classified by him into two categories, called *sama* and *anya* (the "same" and the "other"). The *anya* is also referred to as *viṣama*, as it is contrary to *sama*, and also because it puts us into many troubles. *Viṣama* literally means, that which is difficult and uneven.

Items of knowledge such as, "this is a pot," "this is a pen," etc. are examples of the *anya* (the other) aspect of knowledge. There we see the many. There is something generic in all these numerous items of knowledge. That generic aspect is referred to by the word "this" in the knowledge "this is a pot." It refers to something existing. That existence is given specificity by "pot," "pen," etc.

Though the knowledge "this is a pot" is different from the knowledge "this is a pen," as knowledge they are not different. Each of them is knowledge. Thus, in and through each item of knowledge, we can also say, "this is knowledge." Here multiplicity is reduced to unity. This kind of knowledge is called *sama* (the same). It reduces everything to unity. It also has its generic and specific aspects. Here what is referred to by "this" is the generic, and what by "knowledge" is the specific. This generic "this" in "this is knowledge" is the one unconditional Consciousness that subsists as the material cause for all the functional aspects of knowledge, the totality of which constitutes our life-experience. Narayana Guru suggests that our meditation, in order to attain the ultimate goal of our enquiry, should be centred round this generic Consciousness.[9]

Brahman not Worshippable

Each item of our knowledge is about something external or something internal. We become able to see the unity of Consciousness intuitively when we visualise each item of knowledge as "This is a form of knowledge," "This is another form of knowledge," "This is still another form of knowledge," etc. This one Consciousness that finds

9. See *Ātmopadeśa Śatakam*, verses 36 to 42.

expression in the various forms of experience is the *Brahman* understood here.

That Consciousness is neither internal nor external. It is neither the observer nor the observed. Internality and externality are experienced in this Consciousness. It is not something that can be loved, because the emotion called love is only an expression of that Consciousness. It is not something that can be adored and worshipped, because all such attitudes are only sparks of that great bonfire. That is the reason why it is said, "*Brahman* is not what is adored as something that can be referred to as 'this.'" In other words, the love of the one who knows Reality is not for "this" or "that," but for the entirety.

It is stated in the *Īśa Upaniṣad,*

> He who sees all beings in the Self and the Self in all beings,
> he does not feel any revulsion by the very reason.[10]

In the same way, one who sees all functions in the substratum of one Consciousness and the expression of the one Consciousness in all our experiences, has nothing to love or adore specifically. If there is any, it is the all. Such an attitude of worshipfulness will be extolled in the 31st *mantra* of the present Upaniṣad itself, when it says, *tadvanam ity upāsitavyam* (it is worshippable as *tadvanam*). The implications in the word *tadvanam* will be discussed when we come to that *mantra.*

The next four *mantras* present the same vision, with mind, eye, ear and vital breath, in the place of the speech referred to in the present one. Altogether these *mantras* reveal the truth that *Brahman* is the one Consciousness which is the causal existence, the motivating force for the functional manifestation of all our experiences referred to in the first

---

10. *Īśa Upaniṣad,* 6.

mantra. These *mantras* serve also as a guide for our contemplative search for the ultimate Reality.

यन्मनसा न मनुते येनाहुर् मनो मतम् ।
तदेव ब्रह्म त्वं विद्धि नेदं यदिदमुपासते ॥ ६ ॥

yan manasā na manute yenāhur mano matam ।
tad eva brahma tvaṁ viddhi nedaṁ yad idam upāsate ॥ 6 ॥

That which is not thought of by the mind, but that by which, they say, the mind is thought of, that verily, know thou, is *Brahman*, and not what here is adored as "this."

यच्चक्षुषा न पश्यति येन चक्षूँषि पश्यति ।
तदेव ब्रह्म त्वं विद्धि नेदं यदिदमुपासते ॥ ७ ॥

yac cakṣuṣā na paśyati yena cakṣūṁṣi paśyati ।
tad eva brahma tvaṁ viddhi nedaṁ yad idam upāsate ॥ 7 ॥

That which is not seen by the eye, but by which the eyes are seen, that verily, know thou, is *Brahman*, and not what here is adored as "this."

यच्छ्रोत्रेण न शृणोति येन श्रोत्रमिदं श्रुतम् ।
तदेव ब्रह्म त्वं विद्धि नेदं यदिदमुपासते ॥ ८ ॥

yacchrotreṇa na śṛṇoti yena śrotram idam śrutam ।
tad eva brahma tvaṁ viddhi nedaṁ yad idam upāsate ॥ 8 ॥

That which is not heard by the ear, but by which these ears are heard, that verily, know thou, is *Brahman*, and not what here is adored as "this."

यत् प्राणेन न प्राणिति येन प्राणः प्रणीयते ।
तदेव बह्म त्वं विद्धि नेदं यदिदमुपासते ॥ ९ ॥

yat prāṇena na prāṇiti yena prāṇaḥ praṇīyate ।
tad eva brahma tvaṁ viddhi nedaṁ yad idam upāsate ॥ 9 ॥

That which is not breathed by the vital breath, but by which the vital breath is breathed, that verily, know thou, is *Brahman*; not what here is adored as "this."

2

Section Two

यदि मन्यसे सुवेदेति दभ्रमेवापि
नूनं त्वं वेत्थ ब्रह्मणो रूपम्।
यदस्य त्वं यदस्य देवेष्वथ नु
मीमांस्यमेव ते, मन्ये विदितम्॥ १॥

yadi manyase suvedeti dabhram evāpi
nūnaṁ tvaṁ vettha brahmaṇo rūpam ।
yad asya tvaṁ yad asya deveṣv atha nu
mīmāṁsyam eva te, manye viditam ॥ 1 ॥

If you think that you know that form of *Brahman*, which if you think is known even to gods, that is slight indeed, to be sure. Therefore it has to be deeply reflected on. (After a deep reflection the disciple comes back and says), "I think now I understand."

It is normal in a class for a teacher to ask the student, "Do you follow me?" or "Did you get the point?" The answer may be either "Yes" or "No." The teacher becomes satisfied if the answer is, "Yes." But the *guru* in this teaching process does not become satisfied even with the answer, "Yes." He says, "If you think that you understand it, that form of *Brahman* which you have understood is very slight indeed. If you think that that form is understood even by gods (*deva*s) that also is slight indeed."

Wisdom Cannot be Taught

Everything is usually taught by using words as a medium. Vedānta is not an exception. We have already seen, how words are formulated. In the transcendental Consciousness (*parā*) a visualisable form arises (*paśyantī*). This vision is melted and poured into the mould of a medium (*madhyamā*), which here is a language, and it results in the formulation of the uttered words (*vaikharī*).

These words have as their meaning, the vision of the idea, which is the second stage referred to above. But the transcendental Consciousness is the homogeneous matrix on which all these ideations take place. This matrix is infinite. What a word can do is to convey a finite idea, which is only a spark of the infinite and transcendental Consciousness. So if one thinks of having understood the transcendental Reality or *Brahman*, as the meaning of the words heard from someone, that Reality is only a minute spark of a real infinite Reality, because words do not hold that Reality as their meaning.

As was stated earlier, the Reality is the Speech of all speeches that enables a word to contain some meaning. Therefore, after imparting the subtle aspects of *Brahmavidyā*, as far as words can go, the *guru* warns the disciple that, if he thinks he understood it, what he has understood is only a small spark of a boundless bonfire.

A Vedāntin sees all the newer and newer experiences in life as expressive sparkings of the infinite possibilities inherent in *Brahman*. Whatever is seen, whatever is understood, whatever is experienced, is a minute fragment of the total Reality become manifest. In this sense also it could be said, "This Absolute that you think of as understood by you is only very slight indeed."

The Absolute is attained only as one's Self-realisation. That means, as the experience of one's own enduring existence, awareness and self-contentment. One's own experience of existence is also a spurting of the becoming, that happens in the one Consciousness underlying everything. So the self-experience one has cannot be taken to be the totality of the Absolute. The self-experience is only the experience of a drop of water in the form of its identity with the ocean. It does not comprise the entire ocean. What a drop experiences as its self-content is a little of the ocean. The *guru* here does not say that what the disciple has understood is wrong, but he reminds him that it is only a little of the Reality.

This is not because of any incompetence on the part of the disciple. The *guru* consoles him by saying, even if gods, who are supposed to be far superior to human beings, think that they understood *Brahman*, that *Brahman* is also very slight. That means, the impossibility of knowing *Brahman* as the meaning content of words is only but natural.

How to Get Over

The ultimate aim of any Upaniṣad is not to make the enquirer satisfied with this little knowledge, but it is to lead him to the farthest limit of knowledge. The enquiry as intended by the Upaniṣads is not to be confined to grasping the meaning of the words spoken by a *guru*, or reading and finding out the word-meanings of scriptures. This hearing or reading is only the first step in the process of an ascent. Technically this first step is called *śravaṇa* (hearing) in Vedānta textbooks.

In the *Bṛhadāraṇyaka Upaniṣad*, the Guru Yājñavalkya tells his disciple and wife Maitreyī, that for the final attainment of Self-awareness one has to go through the three stages of *śravaṇa, manana* and *nididhyāsana*. The second step is the cogitation by oneself on what is heard from a *guru*. It is here that we need a critical acumen, scientific clarity, definiteness and structural integrity.

This cogitation is to be supplemented by our meditation or intuitive contemplation. This is called *nididhyāsana*, the last step. The words one hears from a *guru* help only as a foothold for a firm beginning of self-effort. The final attainment is the experience of one's own non-difference from the transcendental (*parā*). In effect, it is the experience of non-difference of everything that has come into being, from the transcendental. In that intuitive experience, the existence (*sat*) of one transcendental Reality is visualised as pervading everything as their content, one transcendental Consciousness (*cit*) as encompassing everything from the microcosmic to the macrocosmic, all into a living whole with a structural integrity, and one Happiness (*ānanda*) or Value as inherent in all the pleasures and pains.

When this experience of identity becomes real, my love for myself becomes extended to everything. The nature of life is then felt to have changed totally. The life, which was being experienced as an ocean of sufferings, turns out to be an ocean of Happiness, or Self-contentment, where birth and death have no meaning. This attainment of immortality is the final goal of an Upaniṣad.

Who Can Get Over

The capability to understand words, to cogitate on their meaning and to have an intuitive vision, could be considered the highest gift of man. Of these three, the role of cogitation or pondering over what was understood from the words, is a vital one because its nature marks the individuality of a person. This ability of man is called *manana*. The word for human beings in Sanskrit is *manuṣya*, which means the descendants of Manu. Manu means one who is capable of doing *manana* or cogitation.

The first section of the *Kena Upaniṣad* is that of hearing the oral instruction or *śravaṇa*. The *guru*, after giving the instruction, turns the attention of the disciple to the necessity of cogitating on it by himself. So he says, "This has to be deeply reflected on."

Even a *guru* is helpless in this cogitation as it has to be done by oneself. The *guru* can only turn the attention of the seeker to the inevitability of one's own cogitation to attain the final conviction. It is here we see how fit a disciple is to attain the final conviction. This fitness of a disciple is called *adhikāra*. Usually the seekers are classified into three groups according to their fitness. The fittest one is called *uttama adhikārī* and the least fit is called *manda adhikārī*. There are some who come in the middle who are called *madhyama adhikārī*. Only the best ones reach the attainment of the final conviction. The middle one will go on the pondering endlessly. The least qualified do not even enter the process of cogitation.

How long it will take to attain the final goal, also depends on the seeker's fitness. No reference is made here as to how long was the disciple's contemplation. He comes back afterwards and says, "Now I think I know the Reality." It is to be naturally presumed, on the ground that all these are presented in the text of a single *mantra*, that the disciple did not take a long period of time and thus he was one of the fittest seekers.

The next *mantra* shows how he expressed his understanding of the ultimate Reality.

नाहं मन्ये सुवेदेति, नो न वेदेति, वेद च ।
यो नस्तद् वेद तद् वेद नो न वेदेति वेद च ॥ २ ॥

nāhaṁ manye suvedeti, no na vedeti, veda ca ।
yo nas tad veda tad veda no na vedeti veda ca ॥ 2 ॥

> "I do not think that I know it well. Nor do I think that I do not know it." "He who among us knows what is meant by this, he knows *Brahman*. It is neither a state of not knowing, nor of knowing."

One who knows *Brahman* sees nothing but *Brahman*. He sees himself as being It. At that state of awareness he is not able to say what It is. What he can do is only to remain silent, overwhelmed by the meaningfulness of It. This is the secret which the disciple realised himself after a prolonged cogitation and meditation.

The disciple comes back to the *guru* and says, "Guru, now I think I know the Reality." But how can it be explained to the *guru*? If it is expalined in any way, it would only be the meaning of some words, and as a result it would only be a little of that total Reality. If he remains silent, it won't be possible to convince the *guru* what he found out. The *guru* must naturally be anxious to know what kind of understanding the disciple has gained.

This state, in which meaningfulness reaches its plenitude so much that words fail to express it, is tackled by the disciple in a very peculiar and subtle way. He says, "I do not think that I know It well. But I do not think that I do not know It either." These words of the disciple satisfy the *guru*. He is convinced that the awareness he wanted to become well founded in the disciple has become really so. This conviction is well indicated by his words which followed: "Only those among us who understand what is meant by this, really know what Reality is."

यस्यामतं तस्य मतं मतं यस्य न वेद सः ।
अविज्ञातं विजानतां विज्ञातमविजानताम् ॥ ३ ॥

yasyāmataṁ tasya mataṁ mataṁ yasya na veda saḥ ।
avijñātaṁ vijānatāṁ vijñātam avijānatām ॥ 3 ॥

> To whomsoever It is not known, to him It is known. To whomsoever It is known, he does not know. It is not specifically understood by those who specifically understand; It is specifically understood by those who do not specifically understand.

Our Sciences

PHYSICS

Man, from the very beginning, has been trying to understand the world in which he lives and also the phenomenon of life. All our sciences are certain facets of this never-ending enquiry. Physics is the science that carries on the enquiry from the side of matter. The range of its field of enquiry is very extensive. At one extreme are the subatomic particles, the movement of which is studied by the branch of physics called quantum mechanics. At the other extreme is astrophysics, where the field of enquiry is the limitlessly expanding universe where millions of galaxies are constantly moving apart from each other.

We have already seen how an undefinability lurks at the core of the physicalness of reality, as is found at both these extremes. The scientist is wonderstruck by finding his own mind as having a place in the object he is observing. So he doubts the possibility of finding out the ultimate reality with the help of modern physics, or at least with the help of the prevailing methods of its enquiry.

CHEMISTRY

Chemistry is the science that studies the interaction between atoms of various elements, that causes the structuring and destructuring of everything in this universe.

The human body and the brain in it are also thought of in this science as a result of such chemical combinations. In spite of all its advancement, chemistry has not been able to show us how the phenomenon of consciousness emerges out of certain chemical combinations. On observing the mental phenomena and the physical phenomena side by side, we become unable to say which is the cause of which. Even the validity of the law of causality appears to be questionable in our search for an ultimate reality.

BIOLOGY

The name Biology itself suggests that it is the science of life. But what is studied in that science is everything concerned with living beings, excepting life. From the chromosomes in living cells, the supposedly physical mechanism for the emergence of life, to the inert hair which also forms part of the living body, everything that belongs to an organism, along with the mutations and evolutions caused to them and caused by them, are all studied under this science. Still the phenomenon called life or consciousness remains a mystery that eludes it.

PSYCHOLOGY

Psychology is the science that claims to study our mental phenomena. It is strange that no text book or encyclopaedia of psychology defines what mind is. The enquiry of psychology into the origin of consciousness has given us nothing more than what biology has done. The chemical changes that take place in the neurons and the resulting physical changes are what this science shows us as the cause of the emergence of consciousness. But this science does not enlighten us on how these physical events are transformed into a non-physical phenomenon called consciousness, and how these changes find their expression through poems, paintings, philosophies, dreams and so on.

We see in a textbook of psychology, in its chapters dealing with the states of mind, only a description of changes that happen to the physical body when we are in such states. The causal relationship between these physical changes and the mental states is still a big question mark within psychology. There is presumption among scientists that everything in this universe is caused by some physical event. Based on it, we assume that mental phenomena are caused by physical changes. But no one has either questioned the above presumption or proved it. Why can't we presume that the physical changes are caused by the mental states? The hearing of some very sad news sometimes causes physical weakness and sometimes even a collapse. That means, mental states could be causal to physical changes. In short, the causal relation between body and mind is a mystery even to the science of psychology.

The known world and the unknown mystery of the universe could be compared to an iceberg. Only a small portion of it is visible or knowable. Its huge body is hidden in the depths of the unknown. Man has developed different sciences to enable him to know the reality. But what he can reach with the help of all these sciences is only the visible portion above the surface. He feels himself at a loss when he finds that the totality of the truth is not understandable with the help of its visible portion alone.

What man knows is only how to relate different aspects of the visible portion above the surface, between themselves, as causes and effects. What he cannot relate as cause and effect belongs to a realm of mystery for him. That which is not a mystery to man is only a very little of this universe and also of life. Everything else is an unknown mystery.

Man thinks there are certain rules which govern our enquiry concerning the visible part of the Reality. He also presumes that these rules are applicable to the unknown depths of the mystery also, and thus wants to plunge into its depths. But, seeing there no sign of any guidance of reasoning, he keeps back, and remains doubtingly on the shore of the depths. In that state what he thinks to have known about the depths, is only an unveiling of a new face of his ignorance. Thus, whoever claims to have known the ultimate Reality specifically with the help of our modern devices of science, could surely be judged as not knowing the Reality. Therefore it is said, "To whomsoever it is known, he does not know."

The Real Knowledge of Reality

There is yet another kind of knowledge. Instead of treating this universe and our life as a mystery with a doubtful attitude, this knowledge acknowledges mystery as the Reality, or the Reality as a mystery. It is unknown and is unknowable. Those who have this knowledge realise that what appears as the universe is a little tip of the great iceberg of this mystery. What we understand as real with the help of our senses, is only this little tip of it. But that little tip does not exist apart from the great iceberg.

We, the enquirers, are also part of that visible little tip, and thus, not different from the great iceberg. Our consciousness, its relation to the physical body, the structural unity of everything, are all part of that great mystery. "I," the enquirer, am only a miniature form of that total mystery. The mystery called "I" and the mystery called the universe are thus not two mysteries. The conviction that "I" and the universe are only two manifest expressions of one Mystery, and one's experience of identity with It, is the culmination of this latter kind of knowledge.

One who knows thus, does not analyse the nature of Reality deductively into different components, with the help of the law of causation, nor synthesize them inductively. What he realises is the meaninglessness of such methods in the realm of the total. But those who stick to those methods, which are relevant only to the visible little tip, might ridicule him as one who knows nothing, as just a believer or even a crackpot. But the Upaniṣad says, such a one who is well aware that he does not know is the one who really knows, or "To whomsoever It is not known, to him It is known."

The Sanskrit equivalent to the modern concept of science is *vijñāna*, which literally means, specific knowledge. All our sciences attempt to know the reality by dividing the little visible tip of the great iceberg, into different fields of enquiry. Each science gives stress to a specific aspect of it. Some of these sciences are again subdivided into various fields of specialisation. This kind of enquiry that concentrates its attention on specific aspects of the little visible portion of Reality and divides it again into special fields, helps only to lead us away from the entirety of Reality, rather than reaching It. So, whatever is known to science is only a little of the total Truth. The more specialized a science is, the farther away we are from the total Reality. The entirety of Reality is never known as a specific item of knowledge. So it is said, "It is not specifically known to those who understand specifically."

But in the case of the latter type of knowledge, the one Reality, which is the unknown, unknowable and infinite Mystery, is realised as existing in and through each of the minute specific aspects of our experience. Whatever is specific in it is only a spark of the infinite fire of Existence. The one who knows thus, knows that the totality of Reality, *Brahman*, is not understandable specifically, but whatever is understandable specifically is a manifest expression of the unspecific *Brahman*. They see the unspecific Reality in and through the specific experiences. Thus, it is specifically understood by them. So it is said, "It is specifically understood by those who do not specifically understand."

> प्रतिबोधविदितं मतममृतत्वं हि विन्दते ।
> आत्मना विन्दते वीर्यं विद्यया विन्दतेऽमृतम् ॥ ४ ॥
>
> *pratibodha-viditaṁ matam amr̥tatvam hi vindate* ।
> *ātmanā vindate vīryaṁ vidyayā vindate 'mr̥tam* ॥ 4 ॥
>
> When that *Brahman* is known in and through every state of consciousness, it is rightly known, for one attains eternal life (by such knowledge). Through one's own self (by oneself) one gains power, and through wisdom one gains immortality.

What is that Reality that is known to one who does not know and unknown to one who knows? We have seen that It is the indwelling and unseen Mind of the mind and Eye of the eye. That is what we call *Brahman*. The contemplation in the last *mantra* was centred round the method of knowing it. Now we turn to its nature and content. We could either say that It has no nature and content of Its own, or that it is Its own nature that we see in everything that appears here phenomenally.

The Eternal and the Transient

We know, the content of an ornament is gold. Gold has no form of its own. It is the existential content that underlies in all the forms of ornaments. An ornament is visible, but gold pure and simple is invisible, because it has no form of its own. That which has no form is always invisible. That means, gold is the invisible substance in the visible form of an ornament.

In Sanskrit the existential content is called *sat* and its manifest form is called *bhāva*. The existential content cannot be made non-existent. But its form could be altered. So the existential content is eternal (*nitya*) and its visible form is transient (*anitya*). The ornament has the eternal and transient aspects in it. The relevance of duality of the eternal and the transient is only in our understanding.

The gold and the ornament have never existed separate. It is a non-dual reality. That means, the eternal gold and the transient form are non-dual in the truth called ornament. Gold can never exist without a form. Form can never exist without a content. When rationally understood, we conceive one reality as having two aspects. If we represent these two aspects as if in a graph for the sake of clarity, the existential aspect could be called the vertical axis, and the transient formal aspect as the horizontal one. The non-dual reality is the meeting point of the two axes.

Let us see *Brahman* in the place of gold and the universe in the place of ornaments. Then, the unknown and unknowable *Brahman* has to be realised in and through every manifest form of existence.

That existence, most intimately and directly experienced by the seeker, would be in the form of one's own being. That means, the eternal *Brahman* is to be realised by the seeker, as his own self (*ātmā*). The essence of such an experience, if put in words, would be, "This self is *Brahman*" (*ayam ātmā brahma*), one of the great dicta (*mahāvākya*s) of Vedānta. It appears in the *Māṇḍūkya Upaniṣad*.[1] Experiencing the self-existence as *Brahman* is not a knowledge that is mediate in nature. It is an immediate awareness. Such an immediate intuitive vision is called *aparokṣa anubhūti* in the textbooks of Vedānta.

Content of the Self

Thus *Brahman* is to be intuitively experienced as one's own self. Now, what is the nature and content of the self? It is unconditioned Consciousness only. Narayana Guru defines

1. *Māṇḍūkya Upaniṣad*, 2.

ātmā (self) as, "What in darkness remains aware, the self indeed that is."[2]

This Consciousness that throbs in us and as us, has also its distinguishable vertical and horizontal factors.

One Consciousness, Many Functions

It is 5 o'clock in the morning. The chiming of the big bell at Śivagiri is re-echoing. I got up. A day begins. The sound of the bell comes from half a kilometre away. How can it wake me up? What is a sound? How did it reach me? How did I get up? I applied force on the bed as I got up. The bed would have broken up, had it not been built strong enough to support my weight and also to withstand the force I apply. Does the strength of the bed increase as I apply force? Not necessarily. If the cot is made strong enough to carry the maximum possible weight and to stand the maximum expected force, we need not worry about its strength. Now I am thinking as a physicist.

How did the chiming of the bell enter me? What are the mechanisms in me to receive the vibrations in the air and to transform them into the experience of hearing a sound? This enquiry of mine is as a biology student.

What is meant by waking up? What was the condition of consciousness before waking up? Consciousness was not functioning before waking up. Just on waking up, I remember the things to be done today, and I get ready to become engrossed in them. How could such a change happen to consciousness? What is memory? How is it formulated and stored up in me? How did I get a sense of responsibilty? I feel responsible only towards people or things that seem evidently meaningful to me. What is that sense of value which makes certain things

---

2. *Ātmopadeśa Śatakam*, v. 27.

meaningful to me and certain others meaningless? Now I am thinking of the problems in psychology.

Didn't all these problems arise in my consciousness? Are not all of these, expressions of my own existence, my own life? What is life? Why is life? Is it not my life that has created all these problems? Who am I? What is it? Now my enquiry is concerning the fundamental problems of life, concerning the ultimate Reality.

We have seen that what we call self is the consciousness that remains aware of itself in a darkness. I am nothing but that consciousness. I forgot one thing in the meanwhile: it was I myself who was thinking as a physics student, as a biology student, as a psychology student, and also as the enquirer into the ultimate Reality. It was one and the same consciousness that was thinking in all these different ways. In other words, one and the same consciousness was expressing itself in all these fields of enquiry. We may say that the one consciousness which functions through all these sciences is the vertical aspect of knowledge or Self, and various sciences are the horizontal manifestations of the same.

When I was asking questions and trying to answer them, I was in complete oblivion that one and the same consciousness was functioning in and through them. Had I been fully aware of that one consciousness, I would have seen my questioning, my attempt to answer them and the evaluation of the answers, as not different from or as identical with that one consciousness. How true are Narayana Guru's words in his composition called *Aṛivu* (Consciousness Examined) when he says:

> Consciousness is not known, but
> When known, both become one.[3]

3. *Aṛivu*, v. 5.

The Non-duality

How can we know the Self or Consciousness except as the homogeneous vertical Reality which subsists in, and finds its own expression in, the various states of mind? These states of Consciousness are only differently modulated versions of that one Reality. The Self becomes "specifically understood" (*vijñātam*) and "properly understood" (*matam*) when its reality is experienced in each and every specific function and state of Consciousness. *Brahman* (the Absolute) is to be experienced as the eternal invisible, indwelling Reality, which is vertical, in each and every actuality of the transactional world, which is horizontal in nature. The intuitive experience of non-duality (*advaita*) is where these two axes meet.

Immortality and Its Attainment

We know, death is inevitable. Still all of us have a longing to be immortal. Nature itself has devised a way as part of our life to make ourselves immortal. It is the procreative power in us to make ourselves immortal through our progeny. This power produces one horizontal and transactional manifestation of the Self from another one. Each of the transactional apparent forms has its own birth and death. But through the eternality of births and deaths, the immortality of the Self becomes real. This is a phenomenon common to all living beings as a natural instinct.

This natural instinct causes no sense of relationship and the resultant entanglements in any of the living beings, except humans. The attachment and the sense of protectorhood a mother has towards her offspring naturally ceases in animals by the time the latter becomes capable of self-supporting. Man alone has created a world of relationships out of this natural instinct, and he finds himself entangled in it forever.

It is really the instinct for attaining immortality that has put him in bondage. But man is not aware of it.

Once in a while a rare human being appears, who finds out this vicious circle man is caught in, and sees that the real attainment of freedom for man could be effected only by releasing him from the entanglements of the relativism that causes it. In other words, after recognising the entanglements he is caught in, man's attainment of immortality is to be realised by his strenuous effort to emancipate himself from relativism. The awareness of the absolute Reality adds to the efficacy of this emancipation from the other side. This absolute Reality, as we have seen, is the Being that is in all the becomings. It is that Being that appears here as the "I" or the self.

The self is experienced as an awareness that, as we have already seen, subsists in all the states of consciousness. To know that it is the one absolute Reality that appears as "I" and my states of consciousness, and to live every moment with this awareness, is called *vidyā* in Sanskrit. Narayana Guru defines *vidyā* thus:

> The non-Self is unreal, the Self is real;
> the means by which such knowledge comes,
> that is *vidyā*, like the recognition
> of the truth about rope and snake.[4]

The present *mantra* of the Upaniṣad says, "Through wisdom (*vidyā*) one gains immortality." When we examine these words keeping all that is stated above in mind, we feel, these words are more than an instruction on a philosophical principle. It becomes our own experience of immortality. This experience and the fearlessness mentioned earlier are not different.

---

4. *Darśanamālā*, IV.3.

Immortality, A living Truth

How can this fearlessness or immortality become a living truth for us? It is not merely a theoretical conviction that is aimed at. The theory or principle has to become transformed as making every living moment of our life meaningful as an experience of immortality. What is needed here is not merely the power of discrimination and intellectual conviction, but also a will power to stick to that conviction in our daily life so as to make it a living truth. In other words, we should have that mental strength to make our actual life a horizontalised version or expression of one Reality. Such a desire for Truth to prevail could be seen as having a force of its own in the prophetic religions like Christianity and Islam. The words of Jesus, "Ye generation of vipers," "verily verily I say unto you" and the like reflect this forcefulness. Islam doesn't even hesitate to wage a war, called *jihād*, to see that Truth prevails. But this aspect is stressed only in a rather mild way in the Eastern philosophies and religions, through words like, "This Self is not attained by a weak-minded one."

This indicates that, knowing the ultimate Reality as understood here implies an intellectual conviction as well as an emotional fervour. Stated otherwise, while seeing the intellectual conviction and the emotional fervour as expressions of one and the same consciousness, our intellectual and emotional identity with the Reality should also be an actuality. This gives us a new kind of strength. It is an inner strength which relies on nothing else and hence is absolutist. One gains that strength from nowhere else, but from oneself. So it is said, "By oneself one gains power."

इह चेदवेदीदथ सत्यमस्ति
न चेदिहावेदीन्महती विनष्टिः।
भूतेषु भूतेषु विचित्य धीराः
प्रेत्यास्माल्लोकादमृता भवन्ति ॥ ५ ॥

iha ced avedīd atha satyam asti
na ced ihāvedīn mahatī vinaṣṭiḥ ।
bhūteṣu bhūteṣu vicitya dhīrāḥ
pretyāsmāl lokād amṛtā bhavanti ॥ 5 ॥

If known here itself, then it is the Truth. If not known here itself, it is a great loss. The wise ones, seeing the Real in all that has come into being here, become immortal on going forward from this world.

We saw in the last *mantra* how the one Self, whose content is Consciousness, is to be visualised as the Reality that appears as the various states of consciousness. That was a vision from the *cit* or Consciousness aspect of the one Reality. Now we turn in the present *mantra* to the *sat* or the existential aspect of the same. Here the one Reality is visualised as the substance that exists in, and manifests itself as, everything that has come into being in this world. Both the visions lead us to the experience of Immortality (*amṛtatva*).

Śaṅkara's View

The Śaṅkara school of Vedānta called *advaita* (non-dualism) considers the appearance of the material world as an illusion caused by *avidyā* or nescience. What we understand as soul (*jīva*) and body (*śarīra*), according to this school, are not real by themselves. Śaṅkara in his composition called *Ātmabodha* (Self-Knowledge) says:

> So long as the world appears to be real, just as the mother-of-pearl appears to be silver, *Brahman*, that is the non-dual basis of everything, will not be understood.[5]

The one Reality appears as many, because it is veiled by the conditionings caused by *avidyā* (nescience). Thus the Śaṅkara

5. *Ātmabodha*, v. 7.

school of Vedānta would naturally interpret the present *mantra* thus: if *Brahman* is understood as the basic Reality, veiled by the superimpositions caused by *avidyā*, that results in the appearance of the phenomenal world here, it is the true knowledge of *Brahman*.

Rāmānuja's View

Vedānta has three basic textbooks, which are the Upaniṣads, the *Bhagavad Gītā*, and the *Brahmasūtras*. They are often called by the common title, the *Prasthāna-traya*. Śaṅkara substantiated his school of Vedānta called *advaita* (non-dualism) through his elaborate commentaries on the above said three basic textbooks. But after a few centuries, another famous thinker wrote commentaries on the very same textbooks and substantiated another school of Vedānta known as *viśiṣṭādvaita* (qualified non-dualism). This school is more theological than philosphical in nature. The gist what of this school teaches is given in the first sentence of the book called *Yatīndra-mata-dīpikā* by Śrīnivāsācāriyar, thus,

> Śrīman Nārāyaṇa (Viṣṇu), qualified by *cit* (souls) and *acit* (matter), is the non-dual Reality. Propitiated by devotion and surrender (*bhakti* and *prapatti*), He himself is the means for the final release (*mokṣa*). Qualified by an extra-natural body, He himself is the ultimate end to be reached.[6]

Just as our souls are qualified by our physical body, Viṣṇu the one ultimate Reality has souls and inert bodies for His auspicious qualities. These two qualities together constitute this universe. The cosmos is thus His body. Just as Viṣṇu is beginningless and endless, his body (souls and matter) is also beginningless and endless. But there is creation, sustenance and destruction going on.

6. *Yatīndramata Dīpikā*, 1.

Creation here means, matter (*acit*) gets changed in form so that the souls could have a body. At the time of the great absorption (*pralaya*) matter remains absorbed in Viṣṇu in the form of darkness (*tamas*). Afterwards, due to an unrestrainable urge, He stirs up this darkness in Himself and makes it recognisable as different from Him. First it becomes the *akṣara* (the imperishable), and then the *avyakta* (the indistinct) and afterwards *vyakta* (the distinct). Out of the *vyakta* came the entire cosmos having specific and generic forms. At the time of absorption, the souls (*cit*) were remaining without bodies and senses, and hence unable to experience happiness or final release. At the time of creation, God gave them bodies and senses to enable them to experience happiness and attain final release. The intellect of the souls that was dormant at the state of absorption was also expanded by Him to enable the souls to find the final release.

Sustenance in the *viśiṣṭādvaita* philosophy means, God enters everything that is created by Him, just as water permeates through the body of a plant, and protects them. To protect means, to remove all the obstacles to the attainment of the final goal, and also to render help for its attainment.

The final goal is different for different kinds of souls. To the souls in bondage (*baddha-jīva*s), the goal is gaining food, shelter and clothing. The obstacles to be removed for them are the troubles from enemies and other living or non-living beings. To the souls desirous of final release (*mumukṣu-jīva*s), the obstacle to be removed is the bondage with worldly affairs. For them the final goal is reaching the abode of God. For the released souls (*mukta-jīva*s) and the eternal souls (*nitya-jīva*s) the obstacle to be removed is the absence of a chance for doing service to God (*kaiṁkarya*). The final goal for them is eternal service to God.

Destruction according to the philosophy of Rāmānuja means, God takes back the bodies and senses from the souls because they were straying from the ultimate aim and were indulging in sensual pleasures. God wants only to save these souls through destruction. So it is only a blessing in disguise. This is just like a loving father puts his straying son under house-arrest. God has given bodies and senses to the souls only to enable them to do offerings to God. If the souls stray from this, God appears there himself to save them. This saving activity of God is what we call death or destruction.

This God, the creator, sustainer and destroyer of the world, lives in Vaikuṇṭha served eternally by the released souls and the eternal souls. At the same time he remains permeated in his own body, i.e., the world consisting of souls and matter, as its controller.

God is thus seen in everything. This would be the sense in which the Rāmānuja school of Vedānta would interpret the words, "If known here itself, then, it is the Truth."

Madhva's View

A third school of Vedānta called *dvaita* (dualism) also was founded based on another commentary on the very same basic textbooks mentioned earlier. Madhva was its founder. According to him, there are two categories of reality called independent (*svatantra*) and dependent (*paratantra*). *Brahman* is the only independent reality. All the souls and nature (*jīva*s and *prakṛti*) are dependent realities.

The independent reality alone is complete in itself, and it is the most auspicious. It is the Reality of all realities, the Eternal of all eternals. It is the efficient cause of all the becoming, appearance and functions. The dependent realities are inert by themselves, but they are also eternal.

Thus *Brahman* or God, souls (*jīvas*) and nature (*prakṛti*) are the eternal realities.

The dependent realities always attain specific forms, and that is the process by which creation takes place. This is a peculiar theory of this school of thought and it is called *parādhīna viśeṣāpti* (dependent attainment of specificity), because this process is fully controlled by God, the independent Reality. According to this theory, creation of the universe did not take place at any particular time. It is an eternal process that goes on beginningless and endless.

The relation of a soul to God is that of an image to its original (*biṁba-pratibiṁba-bhāva*). It is just like the relation between an object and its shadow. The soul depends on the independent Reality for its existence (*sattā*), appearance (*pratīti*) and function (*pravṛtti*).

There are differences among souls, in their inner nature. This difference is called *svarūpa-tāratamya* (comparativeness of inner nature). Three main distinguishable varieties among the souls are, the *mukti-yogya* (qualified for final release), *nitya-saṁsārī* (those in eternal bondage), and *tamo-yogya* (fit for the world of darkness). This comparativeness is the reason for the appearance of different characters among individuals, with varying degrees of goodness and evilness.

Mokṣa or the final release is the state in which a soul becomes fully aware of its dependence on God, and its nature of being an image of which the original is God Himself. When the soul is not aware of its dependence and the original-image-relationship with God, it thinks of itself to be independent. This state is what is known as *avidyā* (ignorance) in this school of thought. The release from this ignorance enables a soul, the image, to see directly its original, i.e., God. That is the transcendental peace, the ultimate happiness. The souls thus released are also dependent on God. What is called creation is only a blessing endowed on souls by God to enable them to attain final release, after maturation and fulfilment of all its *karma*s (actions).

Eight are the functions that go on as willed by God. They are creation (*sṛṣṭi*), sustenance (*sthiti*), dissolution (*saṁhāra*), controlling (*niyamana*), knowledge (*jñāna*), ignorance (*ajñāna*), bondage (*bandha*) and liberation (*mokṣa*). God is the plenitude of *sat*, *cit* and *ānanda* (Existence, Awareness and Bliss). A little bit of these three is in the souls also. Therefore there is a part-whole-relationship also between *Brahman* and souls. *Brahman* is not unknowable, as the non-dualists think. But the plenitude of *Brahman* is not understood by souls. Each one's understanding of God varies according to one's inner qualities. These inner qualities of souls are called *svarūpa-yogyatā*.

The bliss experienced in the state of final release also varies from soul to soul according to the difference in their inner qualities. This difference in the inner joy is called *svarūpānanda-tāratamya*. This bliss of knowing one's own content as Existence and Awareness and its dependence on God, is the final release or *mokṣa*. Though this Bliss varies from person to person, it is not comparable by others because it is merely an inner experience of each individual. But it is certain that there should be a difference in this experience, as we see that the desire for final release and the effort each one makes for its attainment are different in different individuals.

This theory of the comparativeness of Bliss is a new idea brought in by Madhva in Indian philosophy. The concepts of *sālokya* (being with God at a visible distance), *sāmīpya* (nearness to God), *sārūpya* (sameness of form with God), and *sāyujya* (oneness with God), in the context of final release, were taken advantage of by Madhva to support this theory. Even in the state of being united with God, Madhva doesn't see the oneness of the soul and God. There also they retain their distinctness. What Madhva calls *aparokṣa anubhūti,* (intuitive experience) is the soul's direct knowledge of the original form of God whose reflected image he is.

Those who have this kind of experience are called *jīvanmuktas* (the released ones while living). Such souls become engaged in activities even when experiencing the Bliss of intuitive knowledge. Such a one doesn't have any obligatory activity. No one asks him to do anything. But chances for being engaged in some kind of activity as natural course are wide open in this world for such released souls. They find expression in him in the form of *karma* (actions), *jñāna* (knowledge) and *upāsanā* (service to deity). The activities of the released souls are not for any particular benefit. They are ends and means in themselves. Thus, those souls live in this world as mere shadows of God, experiencing the presence of God in them, in a state of Bliss. The words of the present *mantra,* "If known here itself, then, it is the Truth. If not known here itself it is a great loss" would be interpreted by Madhva to mean this state of the released souls.

Narayana Guru's View

Narayana Guru's philosophy visualises the ultimate Reality as pure and unconditioned Consciousness. All our experiences, whether internal or external, have Consciousness as the substance which gives content to them. He substantiates this vision in his *Advaita Dīpikā* (The Lamp of Non-duality) thus:

> Cloth here is thread, which is but
> cotton, and which, in turn,
> Is seen as elemental stuff again;
> thus speculated on and on,
> All these emerge and appear as they are
> from pure Consciousness,

> Like seeming water in a desert land;
> Consciousness alone ultimately exists.[7]

That means, it is Consciousness, the primal cause, which is nothing but the Self, that is being experienced in the form of a material object which appears as if existing externally. In other words, the pure and formless unconditioned Self is never known as it is by anyone directly. On the contrary, if we visualise the primal and imperishable Reality in all that is transient, just as the existence of the imperishable gold in all the transient forms of ornaments, that will be the real Self. The Self here is the vertical reality that exists in all horizontal manifestations. This could be considered as a correction to the notion that the unconditioned and unmanifest Self is a reality that exists somewhere in a transcendental domain. The *Īśa Upaniṣad* also supports this stand poignantly in the verse already quoted.[8]

A seer of the non-dual Truth does not see the actualities and the Reality as two. In other words, there is no room for any kind of duality such as the vertical and the horizontal, *parā* and *aparā* (the transcendental and the immanent), *cit* and *jaḍa* (mind and matter), *iha* and *para* (here and the hereafter), *eka* and *aneka* (one and the many), *vyāvahārika* and *pāramārthika* (actuality and reality), in the one Reality visualised here in the Upaniṣad. All these dual aspects have relevance only as part of our way of approach to the reality and not to the Reality as such. Doctrinally and axiologically, thus, there is no room for any duality, but duality is relied on as a methodological necessity.

The duality that forms only part of the method of enquiry is very often mistaken for a doctrinal duality, and as

---

7. *Advaita Dīpikā*, v. 4.

8. See page 35 above.

a result, a notion that the Reality exists somewhere in a transcendental world becomes fixed. Those who have such fixed ideas, lose not only that transcendental world but the world here also. So it is said in the Upaniṣad, "If not known here itself, it is a great loss."

A Double Gain

Narayana Guru, in his *One Hundred Verses of Self Instruction*, says:

> Apart from knowing this Consciousness here
> By finding oneself not different from the
> very Consciousness,
> One does not know It, confounded by the
> notion of the other;
> Who does see this supreme secret of the wise one?[9]

The Guru makes it very clear in these words that the ultimate Reality is to be seen in our functional knowledge as the Consciousness-content, by knowledge. That is the real content of the "I" in me. That content is the same in all the other beings also. So the one who sees the real "I" sees the same "I" in everyone else and in everything. This awareness of oneness expresses itself in the form of an attitude in which "I" treat the interest of everyone as "my" own interest and this attitude becomes normal to "me." Then "I" have nothing that can be called "mine." Everything is everyone's. Everyone can share it. This is an actual experience of the oneness of Reality, where the words, "If known here itself, then it is the Truth" becomes meaningful as living experience. We gain not only this world and the other in such an experience, but they merge into one also.

Those who do not have this attitude in their life as a normal way of functioning, lose all the happiness in this

9. *Ātmopadeśa Śatakam*, v. 64.

world because of their greed and grudge that go with it, and the resultant enmity and fear, let alone the happiness in the next world, if any. If religions promise any celestial happiness, it will always remain a mere promise.

In the case of he who sees the ultimate Reality (the Self or Consciousness), he sees in everything the same Reality alone, the essence of the Self alone. What he feels towards each one would only be the love for the Self. Life here in this world becomes filled with the meaning of the Self. It becomes lovable and beautiful. The saying "God is Love" or "The Truth is Love" thus becomes an actual experience. Those who know the Reality thus are called *dhīra*s, not in the sense that they are the men of wisdom only, but in the sense that they are absolutely fearless also. They have no "other" to be afraid of, because they see everything as not apart from themselves. They have no suffering and no illusion too. What is experienced is only the Bliss of immortality and fearlessness (*amṛta* and *abhaya*).

Until realising this Truth, one would be under the illusion that the soul would go somewhere after death. On realising the Truth, one is fully convinced that what always exists is only the Self. "The here" and "the hereafter" have no existence apart from the Self. That Self is immortal. I am that Self. That is everything. Everything is immortal. Thus one has freed oneself from the world of death. So it is said, "He becomes immortal on going forward from (or leaving) this world." One who knows the one Imperishable Reality has already left the world of birth and death behind.

3

Section Three

THE wisdom-teaching or the original philosophy of the *Kena Upaniṣad* could be considered as fully covered by the first two sections. The third section is the narration of an episode from the Purāṇas, which is related here to substantiate the philosophy already presented. The episode is that of the war between *deva*s and *asura*s (gods and demons) in which the gods had the final victory. When they won the war they became megalomaniac, assuming that it was because of their greatness that they won the war. So *Brahman*, the one all-underlying and all-controlling Reality, conducted a test on them in order to free gods from their illusion. They failed in the test and finally *Brahman* appeard before the king of gods (Indra) and made him realise that it was really *Brahman* that won the war. Śaṅkara, in his commentary, says, this story is introduced as a part of the Upaniṣad for reasons of exegesis or *arthavāda*.

Arthavāda Revalued

There is a section called Brāhmaṇas in the Vedic literature. It is a critical appreciation of the section dealing with rituals, which shows the usefulness of strictly following the instructions contained in the first part of the Vedas, which prescribe the various rituals. It also states what adverse effects would there be if these instructions are not followed. This is generally supported by various episodes. *Arthavāda* is defined thus in the *Gautama-Sūtras*:

stutir nindā parākr̥tiḥ
purākalpa ity arthavādaḥ ।

Stating the goods arising from the proper observance, and the evils arising from its omission, and also adducing historical instances in its support is called *arthavāda*.

The aim of *arthavāda* is to slight any tendency that wells up against Vedic rituals.

According to Laukākṣī Bhāskara, *arthavāda* can be of three types, namely *guṇavāda, anuvāda, bhūtavāda*. Pointing out the merits of strictly adhering to the Vedic instructions (*vidhi*s) is called *guṇavāda*. This, of course, includes the evils arising from the error of omission also. Repeating the same by way of explanation is called *anuvāda*. Presenting before us all the facts and figures to substantiate it, is called *bhūtavāda*. When Śaṅkara says that the third part of the *Kena Upaniṣad* is by way of exegesis, he doesn't make it clear, to which of these three types it belongs.

Generally speaking, *arthavāda* doesn't belong to Vedānta proper which teaches wisdom only, where no necessity of an exegesis arises. *Arthavāda* is relevant only in the section dealing with rituals. But sometimes we come across contexts in which some ritualistic concepts are brought forward into the Upaniṣads, and revalued and given a broader meaning acceptable to the wisdom context. The concept of *arthavāda* itself may be treated as brought forward here to the Upaniṣad and made use of to substantiate the wisdom teaching already given.

The entire world is an eternal flux. There is nothing that does not form part of it. Our attempt to understand the Reality behind the appearance of the world, the present study included, is all part of that flow. There are living and non-living beings in the system of this flow. Among the living beings, there are beings with free will and without free will.

The ones with free will are called human beings. Some scriptures presume the existence of gods (*devas*) in the heaven, who are superior to human beings. Hence they also have to be assumed as having free will.

In the progression of his life as a part of the eternal flux, man attempts to fulfil his desires by following his free will, engaging himself in chosen activities. He experiences a joy when those activities are fulfilled. But when he finds obstacles to their fulfilment, or when the expected result is not achieved, he feels despair. On the other hand, he feels a kind of self-esteem on the fulfilment of his own project. But the one who sees one's own wilful activities and their results, whether favourable or unfavourable, as part of the eternal flux, is neither overjoyed nor desponded at their results. He sees only the unfoldment of the hidden aspects of the eternal flow, in his own activities and their results. Thus he always remains free and detached while being engaged in all his natural activities.

All the activities and their results, both favourable and unfavourable, only add to the wholeness of the eternal flow. There is no success and failure in that wholeness. These are only relative concepts, having relevance only where individuals and their personal interests are counted. Who controls this eternal flow where the wills and the interests of individuals are not counted? We may either say that it is not controlled by anyone, or that it is self-controlled. We may also say that *Brahman* is the controller. Only the will of *Brahman* prevails. The wills and interests of individuals become one with that of *Brahman*. Whether men, gods or demons, this truth is applicable to all.

The teaching of the present Upaniṣad is centred round the problem, "Who controls all the functions going on in the world?" As we have already seen, the one Reality that is the source of all the activities, is not to be seen somewhere else, but should be seen as being in everything that is here and that happens here.

It is easy to learn this as a theory, but we forget it when we are engaged in our routine life. There we emerge again as agents of actions and become attached to their results. We esteem ourselves in our successes, and curse ourselves in our failures, and forget all about *Brahman* that we learnt about. This failure happens not only to humans but even to gods. All the philosophizing we did in the former two sections would become meaningless if we do not make this good, deliberately.

A philosophy is meant not just for philosophising. Its value is when it is lived in our actual life, by finding the ultimate Value of the one Reality in every activity. That is how it is to be realised. The episode narrated here directs our attention to that aspect, showing at the same time the difficulties we would have to face when we try to realise the one Reality in our actual life.

ब्रह्म ह देवेभ्यो विजिग्ये, तस्य ह ब्रह्मणो विजये देवा अमहीयन्त।
त ऐक्षन्तास्माकमेवायं विजयोऽस्माकमेवायं महिमेति ॥ १ ॥

brahma ha devebhyo vijigye, tasya ha brahmaṇo vijaye devā amahīyanta ।
ta aikṣantāsmākam evāyaṁ vijayo 'smākam evāyaṁ mahimeti ॥1 ॥

Brahman, it is said, (once) conquered for the gods, and thus the gods attained glory in the victory of that *Brahman*. The gods thought, "Ours indeed is this victory and ours indeed is this greatness."

One of the central events in almost all the Purāṇas (legends) of India is the war between the gods and the demons (*deva*s and *asuras*) for the possession of *amṛta* (the elixir of immortality). The same episode is brought in here in the Upaniṣad to substantiate the wisdom that was imparted in the first two sections which also aims at attaining immortality. Everyone knows that it was the gods who won the war. We'll also have a preference for the gods to win the war, when we go through the story in the Purāṇas. This is because of the difference we feel in the character of the gods and the demons. While the gods stand for the good the demons stand for the evil.

The Good and the Evil

The problem of good and evil arises from the universal desire for happiness, the most forceful and basic urge that pushes life forward. Each and every living being strives at every moment to attain happiness in one way or another. The longing for happiness is as basic in everyone else as in me. So, if what I do for my self-happiness hinders another's, that deed is against the ultimate Truth. In the case of one who remembers in his actual life that what we call "I", "you" and "he" are all only various manifest forms of one and the same Self, what one does for one's own happiness will always be of such a nature that it ensures the happiness of others also. Such is the criterion for an absolutist morality.

The notions of good and evil are the creations of human interest and free will. Our morality always remains relative when we are guided by our relative interests. When our interest gains an absolutist dimension, i.e., when our personal interests and the interests of the entire system of life coalesce, our life becomes founded on our absolutist morality, to be sure. Having an absolutist morality means, our point of view becoming that of *Brahman* or the Absolute. From the point of view of *Brahman*, the one source of everything that happens here, there is no good and evil. Its creative urge manifests itself undefinably. Certain aspects of that process are just counted as good, and certain others as evil by human beings.

We cannot claim that *Brahman* had an intention that the gods should win the war and that the demons should be defeated. The goodness of gods and the evilness of demons are only relative and conditional. *Brahman* may be said to represent that pure morality which is beyond human goodness and evilness. It is that pure morality, or amorality, that always prevails and wins. What is relatively called the victory of gods and the defeat of demons, forms only a minute part of the total creative process. But this truth was not known to the gods. They live in a world of relative merits and morality, though in heaven. Righteousness and its merits are meaningful there.

What always prevails and wins is only *Brahman*, the Absolute. And what is great is always *Brahman*. Each one of us achieves greatness in our relative life because of that greatness. When this greatness is reflected in human life in its pure form, it appears as an individual's activities which ensure one's own happiness and also that of others at the same time. This may be considered as the absolutist goodness in human life. Whatever done otherwise is evil.

Greatness — Relative and Absolutist

The word *deva* means one who is brightness in essence, and it is also the name of the denizens of heaven as well as of our senses. The senses are called *deva*s because it is the brightness of an awareness that becomes evident in every sensation. The denizens of the heaven such as Indra, Varuṇa, Agni, Mitra, Vāyu, etc. are called *deva*s as they are conceived as the deities or aspects of the universal consciousness that control universal phenomena, like rain, ocean, fire, air, etc. Thus, *deva*s or gods represent consciousness both in its specific and generic aspects as related to different phenomena. That is the reason why we naturally have a preference for the *deva*s to win the war. Of course, the *deva*s did win, according to the stories. But the real victory was not of the *deva*s, but of *Brahman*. This does not mean that *Brahman* had a special liking for the *deva*s nor that he helped them to win over the *asura*s. Everything simply happens as a part of the total scheme that belongs to the greatness (*mahimā*) of *Brahman*.

Mahimā means the quality of being adorable. *Brahman* is the only absolutely adorable reality. It is through *Brahmavidyā* (the Science of the Absolute) that one is promoted from the world of relative greatness and adorability to that of the absolutist greatness and adorability, as will be stated in the *mantra*s 28 and 29. The meaninglessness of the self-esteem of *deva*s will also become evident in the above *mantra*s. The victory and greatness of *Brahman* and of the *deva*s are so sharply contrasted here that the discrimination between relative and absolutist goodness and evilness, between relative victory and defeat and absolutist ones, between relative greatness and meanness and the absolutist ones, becomes evident.

Devas and Asuras in us

*Deva*s and *asura*s waged the war to get possession of the *amr̥takuṁbha* (the pot of the elixir of immortality). *Deva*s, *asura*s and *amr̥takuṁbha* are only symbols which were knit into the stories of the Purāṇas.

*Deva*s and *asura*s represent our own innate traits. Each of us has an attitude which wants to stick to goodness. Another trait in us would be dragging us away to evilness. These two tendencies are represented as *deva*s and *asura*s in the legends of India. At a certain time we become biased to one side, and at another time to the other. This wobbling of our attitude makes us restless. It is then that we search for some ultimate value that makes life meaningful and peaceful. That value which we are seeking is immortal (*amṛta*), symbolized by the *amṛta-kuṁbha* of the stories.

The emergence of this immortal value happens as a result of the intense churning of all the values, or likes and dislikes, of our life. These countless values are symbolised by the milk ocean of the story. The churning happens as a result of the forceful pull of our interest and loyalty to the brighter values represented by the *deva*s on the one side, and the pull of the demonic tendencies in us on the other side, represented by the *asura*s. A turmoil takes place in our psyche as a result of it, which results in the final emergence of the wisdom of the immortal Reality represented by the pot of nectar. Gaining this Reality makes our life immortal. It makes life an experience of fearlessness and peacefulness.

But we assume, even this gaining of wisdom is because of our ability and goodness. It makes us self-conceited. So long as we are so, we are far away from the real Truth. It doesn't become our life. It would remain merely a means for our self-conceit. Therefore, the freedom from such self-conceit is an essential part of our Self-enquiry. That is why the Guru Narayana, as part of his philosophical speculation, prays, "O grant the boon that it may not swell the ego."[1]

Only when we are free from such self-conceit and ego, can the leaving of this world and the reaching of the world of immortality become a reality while living here, as indicated in *mantra* II.5 above.

तद्धैषां विजज्ञौ, तेभ्यो ह प्रादुर्बभूव। तन्न व्यजानत किमिदं यक्षमिति ॥ २ ॥

---

1. *Ātmopadeśa Śatakam*, verse 12.

taddhaiṣāṁ vijajñau, tebhyo ha prādur babhūva । *tan na vyajānata kim idaṁ yakṣam iti* ॥ 2 ॥

Brahman indeed knew this conceit of theirs. He appeared before them, it is said. But they did not know, what adorable *yakṣa* it was.

Brahman found that the *deva*s were self-conceited in their victory, as they were living in the world of relative understanding. Still they could be saved from it. That is why *Brahman* decided to appear before them. The *deva*s saw him only as a *yakṣa*. *Yakṣa* means something adorable and yet unknown.

Visible but Unknown

When we do something with a particular end in view and attain its fulfilment, we do not usually have concern for the unknown force that leads our activity to the end we expect. But we start thinking of that force when our plans fail unexpectedly, because we want to know whose will prevails over ours. No philosophizing is needed for the populace to believe that all this is the sport of God. But what do we know of God? We can only say, it is a great wilful force that can make our wills nothing. So it is adorable. All this is implied in the name *yakṣa*.

It is a wilful force in me and also in the minutest particle of this universe, that controls and integrates everything into one whole. So it is great. Yet we don't know anything about it. At the same time we experience its presence directly as the one will power that controls the entire cosmic system. Thus, when we say that we don't know God, it is as if we say we cannot see that which is just in front of us. This is the plight of the common man. *Deva*s are also not an exception in this respect. They did not see *Brahman* as *Brahman* when He appeared before them. They saw Him as an unknown yet adorable spirit (*yakṣa*) just as any common man might. The Upaniṣad does not say that *Brahman* "appeared" before them in the form of a *yakṣa*. But the *deva*s "saw" Him as a *yakṣa*.

We also Don't See the Reality

According to the episode represented here, the gods seek to know *Brahman* not when they met with any tragedy in life. On the other hand, on their victory over the *asura*s they became self-conceited, and in order to correct them and to show them who always wins, *Brahman* appeared before them. But they could not recognise it as *Brahman* but only as something unknown yet adorable. This is what happens to us also. Even when what we see in the form of the mysterious world before our eyes is nothing but *Brahman,* we think that *Brahman* is something unknown, existing somewhere and yet adorable. As in our case, the *deva*s also did not have the descriminative power to see *Brahman* in what appears to be real. They thought it was a *yakṣa*. Finally, the conundrum also becomes dissolved when they realise that what they took to be a *yakṣa* was *Brahman* itself.

As we have already seen at the end of the last section, the knowers of *Brahman* see only *Brahman* in whatever appears before them, and even in them. That is how the paradox and conundrum lurking at the heart of the knowledge of *Brahman* dissolves, and the experience of immortality becomes real. The reference to *Brahman*'s appearing before the *deva*s and their taking it as a *yakṣa* have to be understood in the light of all this. Though we are seeing *Brahman* Itself in the form of the world before us, we take the world in itself as reality. On realising the unreality of the world we start searching for the reality behind it.

The only Saviour

No one else can save us from the danger, if we are self-conceited in our knowledge. The very same knowledge is the only saving force. In other words, *Brahman* or God Himself has to come as our saviour. Believers take it as a lesson taught by God Himself. The *deva*s became self-conceited on getting possession of the elixir of immortality. What is really immortal is *Brahman*. The very same immortal Reality comes to save them from their self-conceit. But when it appeared before them they saw it only as a *yakṣa*, some unknown but adorable spirit. The apparent world admittedly seems mysterious to us; so is *Brahman*, its source, also.

तेऽग्निमब्रुवन्, जातवेद, एतद् विजानीहि किमेतद् यक्षमिति; तथेति ॥ ३ ॥

te 'gnim abruvan, jātaveda, etad vijānīhi kim etad yakṣam iti; tatheti ॥ 3 ॥

They (the gods) said to Agni, the Fire-god: "O Jātavedas, please find out what this *yakṣa* is." He said, "Let it be so."

तदभ्यद्रवत्, तमभ्यवदत् कोऽसीति, अग्निर्वा अहमस्मीत्यब्रवीज्जातवेदा वा अहमस्मीति ॥ ४ ॥

tad abhyadravat, tam abhyavadat ko 'sīti, agnir vā aham asmīty abravīj jātavedā vā aham asmīti ॥ 4 ॥

He hastened towards *Brahman*. *Brahman* asked him: "Who are you?" Agni said: "I am Agni, indeed. I am known as *jātavedas*."

The Fire-god Agni is chosen as the representative of the *deva*s to go and find out who the *yakṣa* is, and Agni shows his self-esteem before *Brahman*. That is the gist of these *mantra*s.

The Special Place of Agni

Agni has a special status among gods. Life becomes worth living for humans only because there is a hope for the achievement of whatever is considered valuable. Gods are the symbols of these values. The efforts and sufferings man has to endure to achieve these values are symbolised by the fire-sacrifice, the Vedic ritual. Agni or the Fire-god is supposed to be the carrier of offerings. Thus, we may say, the gods depend on human beings for their existence. This dependence of gods on men is represented by the concept in the Vedas that *deva*s have as their food the offerings made by men in fire-sacrifices and carried to them by Agni. *Deva*s, on receiving these offerings, become satisfied and bless the human beings and see to the fulfilment of their desires. The lives of gods and men thus become mutually dependent. Agni plays the role of a common link in this mutual dependence.

Men live in the world here and *deva*s in the other-world. The one who serves as a common link should know both the worlds properly. So Agni is treated as the symbol of knowledge also in the Vedic context. What makes life meaningful, by linking man with the achievement of his aspiration, is knowledge. That could be how Agni got the name *jātavedas*, which means one who knows everything that is born. He is chosen as the rightful person to go to find out who the *yakṣa* is, because he is *jātavedas*. But the omniscience of Agni is restricted to the world of those who are born. It doesn't work in the domain of the knowledge concerning the unborn and imperishable *Brahman*.

Why Agni Fails

There is no place for ego in the knowledge of the Absolute or *Brahmavidyā*. What links man with the achievement of his aspirations is knowledge. One who aspires also thinks, "I am the knower." The omniscience of Agni is, therefore, conditional. The *Brahmajñāna* or the wisdom of the Absolute is that awareness where the knower himself merges with total awareness and loses his individualhood. It goes without saying that the ego, or the sense of being a knower, that is normal with ordinary knowledge, would always be detrimental to such a wisdom.

It is evident here that Agni is not competent enough to attain the knowledge of the *yakṣa*, the unknown yet adorable Reality. On seeing his self-admiring approach, *Brahman* wanted to show him his own inability and dependence. So he asks him, "Who are you?" Agni's answer was in the form of boasting. So the next two *mantras* show how Agni was convinced of his incapability, and how he had to withdraw himself from the search.

तस्मिँस्त्वयि किं वीर्यमित्यपीदँ सर्वं दहेयं यदिदं पृथिव्यामिति ॥ ५ ॥

tasmiṁs tvayi kiṁ vīryam ity apīdaṁ sarvaṁ daheyaṁ yad idaṁ pr̥thivyām iti ॥ 5 ॥

He asked, "What power exists in you?" Agni said, "I can burn everything whatever is on the earth."

तस्मै तृणं निदधावेतद् दहेति, तदुपप्रेयाय सर्वजवेन तन्न शशाक दग्धुं, स तत एव निववृते, नैतदशकं विज्ञातुं यदेतद् यक्षमिति ॥ ६ ॥

tasmai tr̥ṇaṁ nidadhāv etad daheti, tad upapreyāya sarva-javena tanna śaśāka dagdhuṁ, sa tata eva nivavr̥te, naitad-aśakaṁ vijñātuṁ yad etad yakṣam iti ॥ 6 ॥

He placed a blade of grass before him saying, "Burn this." He went towards it with all speed, but could not burn it. He withdrew immediately and said (to the *devas*), "I have not been able to find out what this *yakṣa* is."

Agni is convinced here of his two inabilities. The first one is that the ability to do what he likes is not his own. Secondly, he becomes aware of his inability to know the unknown Reality. So long as one has self-conceited understanding about oneself, the knowledge of the ultimate Reality remains a mirage for him or her. The Truth becomes evident when one's own nature and content are well understood. In fact, self-knowledge itself is the knowledge of *Brahman.* There is a double loss when there is illusory knowledge and a double gain where there is understanding of the Reality.

Two Apsects of Knowledge

Narayana Guru, while making an analytical study of knowledge, categorises the endless powers of knowledge into two types. They are called *sama* (the same) and *anya* (the other) by him. *Sama* is that knowledge which sees only one reality. When many are seen it is called *anya*. If the *sama* could be considered as the vertical aspect of knowledge, *anya* would be its horizontal correlate.

The movement of fire is upward. Its function is to consume everything and reduce the many to one. In that sense, fire represents the *sama* or vertical aspect of knowledge. Ignoring the many and valuing only the oneness would mislead us away from the actualities of life. A real philosopher sees the oneness of these two aspects in the neutrality of consciousness, and realises the ultimate by finding one's own existence in it. That is why Agni failed in knowing *Brahman.* He represents only one of the aspects of knowledge. The other aspect is represented by Vāyu, the god of air, in the following *mantras*. He also could not find out who the mysterious *yakṣa* was, and had to withdraw, just like Agni.

अथ वायुमब्रुवन्, वायवेतद् विजानीहि किमेतद् यक्षमिति; तथेति ॥ ७ ॥

atha vāyum abruvan, vāyav etad vijānīhi kim etad yakṣam iti;
tatheti ॥ 7 ॥

Then they said to Vāyu, the Air-god, "O Vāyu, find it out — what this *yakṣa* is." He said, "Let it be so."

तदभ्यद्रवत्, तमभ्यवदत् कोऽसीति, वायुर्वा अहमस्मीत्यब्रवीन्मातरिश्वा वा अहमस्मीति ॥ ८ ॥

tad abhyadravat, tam abhyavadat ko'sīti, vāyur vā aham asmīty abravīn mātariśvā vā aham asmīti ॥ 8 ॥

He hastened towards the *yakṣa*. It asked him, "Who are you?" He said, "I am Vāyu, indeed. I am known as Mātarīśvān."

The *deva*s must have felt the *yakṣa* to be all the more mysterious when Agni withdrew from the scene, being unable to find out what it was. That might be why they approached Vāyu (the God of Air), the eternal friend of Agni, but able to reach everywhere. Because of this special capability Vāyu is also called *sarvatraga* (one who reaches everywhere). Vāyu might have been quite confident of his ability to reach even the *yakṣa*, in the capacity of his *sarvatraga*. So he agreed to go on the mission in which Agni had failed.

He was asked by the *yakṣa* the same question, in order to subdue his egotism. Vāyu has another quality as Mātarīśvān. Mātarīśvān means one who goes into one's own mother. Space is considered the mother of air. The movement of air is in the same space. In this sense Agni is also often called Mātarīśvān. The mother of fire is fuel. Fire enters the very same fuel and annihilates it.

Vāyu may be considered as representing the reasoning faculty or intelligence in us. Its function is to reach everywhere and examine everything in detail. Thus it corresponds to the *anya* (the other) aspect of knowledge as already mentioned. Its function is of spreading out. The movement of air is sidewards while that of fire is upward. The most popular way of approaching truth is by going into every detail and adding them together to comprehend the totality. This method of approach, in modern times, is known as logical positivism. The failure of Vāyu to find out who the *yakṣa* was, may be taken as indicating the inadequacy of this method to attain the absolute Reality.

तस्मिँस्त्वयि किं वीर्यमित्यपीदँ सर्वमाददीय यदिदं पृथिव्यामिति ॥ ९ ॥

tasmiṁs tvayi kiṁ vīryam ity apīdaṁ sarvam ādadīya yad idaṁ pṛthivyām iti ॥ 9 ॥

He asked Vāyu, "What power exists in you?" Vāyu replied, "I can blow off everything whatever is on the earth."

तस्मै तृणं निदधावेतदादत्स्वेति, तदुपप्रेयाय सर्वजवेन, तन्न शशाकादातुं, स तत एव निववृते नैतदशकं विज्ञातुं यदेतद् यक्षमिति ॥ १० ॥

tasmai tṛṇaṁ nidadhāv etaḍ ādatsveti, tad upapreyāya sarva-javena, tanna śaśākādātuṁ, sa tata eva nivavṛte naitad aśakaṁ vijñātuṁ yad etad yakṣam iti ॥ 10 ॥

He placed a blade of grass before him and said, "You blow this off." Vāyu went towards it with all speed, but could not manage to blow it off. He immediately withdrew and said to the *devas*, "I have not been able to find out what the *yakṣa* is."

Brahman asks the same question to Vāyu as in the case of Agni in order to subdue his self-conceit. What Vāyu declared as his special skill was the ability to blow off everything on the earth. But he also was convinced of his inability to blow off everything as he wished, and also to know the unknown *yakṣa*. Unless *Brahman* decides it, Vāyu or any other element of nature cannot function. In other words, nothing in this world has an independent function other than as part of a total system.

Though Agni and Vāyu are depicted as self-conceited gods, what is intended here concerns us. Our self-conceit is always a hindrance to the acquisition of the real knowledge as intended by the Upaniṣads. Whether the self-conceit is in the name of one's understanding of principles or of worldly matters, both are obstacles to the realisation of the ultimate Reality.

अथेन्द्रमब्रुवन्, मघवन्नेतद् विजानीहि, किमेतद् यक्षमिति; तथेति;
तदभ्यद्रवत्; तस्मात् तिरोदधे ॥ ११ ॥

athendram abruvan, maghavann etad vijānīhi, kim etad yakṣam iti; tatheti; tad abhyadravat; tasmāt tirodadhe ॥ 11 ॥

Then they said to Indra, "O, Maghavan, you find out what this *yakṣa* is." He said, "Yes. Let it be so." He hastened towards it, but it disappeared from before him.

A New Indra

The *devas* had no other way, when Agni and Vāyu withdrew from the scene, than going to Indra, their king, and requesting him to find out who the *yakṣa* was. The superiority of Indra among the gods belongs to the Vedic context. Indra of the Vedas is a hedonist. He never gets satisfied in worldly or rather heavenly pleasures. But the Indra posited here belongs to a revised context of Vedānta.

Devas are the ones whose nature and content are mere brightness. That means knowledge. The Indra presented here is the chief among them. That means he is competent to attain the highest wisdom. His main weapon is *vajra* (thunderbolt), whose nature is also of a radiant brightness. No other weapon is equal to it. That weapon is nothing but the knowledge of all knowledges. In other words, Indra is able to go beyond the duality of the *sama* and *anya* aspects of knowledge. Such an Indra is now about to learn that the *yakṣa* is nothing but *Brahman*.

This revised version of the superiority of Indra, and also of gods among seekers, will be stated in *mantras* 27 and 28.

Maghavan

The epithet "Maghavan" of Indra is stressed here. The word means the strong one. Indra's strength in this context cannot merely be his bodily strength. Had it been so, the vision of *Brahman* that he is going to have would not happen. *Brahmajñāna*, or the wisdom of the Absolute, requires a special strength on the part of the seeker. The *Muṇḍaka Upaniṣad* categorically says, "This wisdom is not attainable by ones who lack strength."[2] The same strength must have made Indra a *maghavan*. It must be the inner strength in taking a unitive or dialectical approach to Reality.

We see the best example of an Indra acceptable to the Upaniṣadic context, in the *Aitareya Upaniṣad* thus:

> He (*Brahman*), thus having born (as the world), perceived the emerged beings; for what else here would one desire to speak? He perceived this very person, *Brahman*, all-pervading; "I have seen it." He said.
>
> Therefore his name is Idandra. Indeed, Idandra is the name. Of him who is Idandra, they speak cryptically as Indra. Gods appear indeed to be fond of the cryptic.[3]

The word "Indra" has an indirect cryptical meaning, as indicated in the *Aitareya Upaniṣad*. It is Idandra who is cryptically called Indra. One who pervades whatever that can be referred to as "this" (*idam*), and then looks back at them to see only oneself in them, is to be called "Idandra." That means, Idandra is that wisdom in which one sees oneself in everything. Here, in the *Kena Upaniṣad*, Indra is just going to become an Idandra. He is therefore called "Indra" in advance.

In the Vedas, Indra is the chief of the *deva*s as their pleasure-loving and *soma*-drinking king. Here in Vedānta also he is given primacy in the sense that he was the one who saw

---

2. *nāyam ātmā balahīnena labhyaḥ* — *Muṇḍaka Upaniṣad*, III.ii.4.
3. *Aitareya Upaniṣad*, I.iii.13.

Brahman directly. Indra thus gains a revalued superiority here. That means, a Vedic concept is revalued and made acceptable to the wisdom context of Vedānta in a revised sense.

Why the Yakṣa Disappears

Brahman spoke directly to Agni and Vāyu when they approached him, and their self-conceit was rooted out. But when Indra did approach him He just disappeared. Why is it so? The ignorant conceive of the unknown ultimate Reality or God as if having a form like everything else. God always remains an unknown and adorable wonder for them. Yet they fear that no favour would be gained in life without His grace. So they conceive of Him as having a concrete form and go to their abodes as pilgrims seeking his favours. They return from such holy places after having "seen" God in his concrete form, fully satisfied. Even at this state of satisfaction they are completely ignorant of the real nature of God. Their returning from holy places after seeing God is therefore just like the withdrawal of Agni and Vāyu after seeing the *yakṣa*, but not knowing him. But there is one difference: Agni and Vāyu knew that they could not find out the real nature of *Brahman*. Those who go to holy places and return satisfied, think they have seen God directly.

But there are some who are real seekers. Through an intensive contemplative effort, known as *tapas*, they try to attain Reality. The first thing that comes to their notice, when they approach Reality, is that It has no form. Every form that was thought to be of Reality becomes meaningless, and disappears. This is represented here as the disappearance of the *yakṣa* when Indra approached Him. Indra is thus going to realise that what he has been seeing as having a form has really no form.

स तस्मिन्नेवाकाशे स्त्रियमाजगाम बहुशोभमानामुमा॰हैमवतीं;
ता॰होवाच, किमेतद् यक्षमिति ॥ १२ ॥

sa tasminn evākāśe striyam ājagāma bahuśobhamānām umāṁ haimavatīṁ; tāṁ hovāca, kim etad yakṣam iti ॥ 12 ॥

In the same region of the sky Indra came upon a lady, the most beautiful Umā, the daughter of Himavān. He asked her, "Who is this *yakṣa*?"

Disappearance of the World of Sufferings and the Emergence of Reality

What appeared to be a mysterious entity has disappeared. And in its place has appeared the most beautiful Umā, the daughter of the Himālayas. Indra must have remained at the spot where the *yakṣa* disappeared, contemplating on its mystery. When Indra was thus found very earnest in his desire and competent to know the Reality, *Brahman* Itself appeared before him as the Goddess of wisdom, Umā. We have already seen how, when a true seeker reaches the Reality, the form it seemed to have disappears. When God becomes formless, the form of the world created by God also is subjected to a basic change. Something new has to emerge in the place of the old. The world becomes not different from that formless Reality. In the place of a world full of problems, what is seen is the grandeur of God or the Absolute. It is the realisation of *Brahman* here and now, that is indicated in the present *mantra*. The true seeker sees the splendour of Reality in the same place where the mysterious world disappeared. So it is stressed here, "in the same region of the sky" (*tasmin eva ākāśe*).

When the world was seen as mere world, it was the abode of endless sufferings. But, when seen as the playful manifestation of the one Reality, all the sufferings just disappear, and in its place the beatitude of the Self alone is experienced. The visual aspect of that beatitude is beauty. So allegorically it is stated here, it appeared in the form of Umā, the most beautiful daughter of Himavān, reminding us of the story of Śiva and Pārvatī.

Umā as a Guru

Indra is in a vacuity here. The Reality that seemed to have a form has disappeared, because Reality as such never becomes visible. Then, how is one to visualise the invisible Reality? Here the Reality itself has to play the role of a living *guru* to teach the secret of this wisdom. That is why, in India, a *guru* and *Brahman* are equated, and a *guru* is given all the respect due to God. Umā, who appeared here, plays the role of a *guru*.

Why a Female Guru?

Why did *Brahman* appear as a *guru* in a female form? The absolute Reality as a principle remains in the world of ideas. In that sense its content is of the nature of knowledge which in Indian philosophy is referred to as *cit*. Such a pure principle never plays the role of a *guru*. Only a concretely existing *guru*, an embodiment of the Reality, can function as an actual *guru*. This existential aspect is referred to as *sat* in Vedānta.

It is through the emergence of newer and newer forms that life continues eternally. In this process of eternal creativity, the female plays the role of the existential (*sat*) aspect. In the visualisation of the ultimate Reality also, its existential aspect is poetically imagined to be a female.

The concepts of *prakṛti* and *puruṣa* (Nature and Spirit) in the Sāṁkhya system of philosophy, and the Śiva and Śakti of the Śākteya system, have also these ideas behind them.

Even in Vedānta, *māya* is sometimes considered a female principle.

Why the Daughter of the Himālayas?

Why should that female be the daughter of the Himālayas? It was the *deva*s who wanted to know who the *yakṣa* was. But they failed in their attempt as it was beyond their capability to know. The *deva*s belong to the Vedic context. But the goddess Umā has no place in the Vedas. The Vedas and the *deva*s are part of the culture of the Aryans who invaded India in ancient times. But there was a pre-Aryan culture in India, which gave primacy to wisdom and its disciplines while the Vedas gave primacy to mere rituals. Umā and her father Himālaya belong to that context.

The Upaniṣads are the outcome of a correction and revision conferred on Vedism as a result of its blending with the pre-Aryan culture. This process took centuries to complete. The mere reference, thus, to the emergence of the beautiful form of Umā Haimavatī provides us with a complete picture of the reculturing and the revaluing process that lasted for centuries in India. The Upaniṣads, the most beautiful flowers of the tree of Indian wisdom, were the result of this long process in history. We could find numerous such indications in different parts of various Upaniṣads. The context of Pravāhaṇa Jaivāli, a kṣatriya, teaching a brāhmaṇa Āruṇi, and the heavenly Ṛṣi Nārada being taught by Sanatkumāra, are other such instances.

4

Section Four

सा ब्रह्मेति होवाच; ब्रह्मणो वा एतद् विजये महीयध्वमिति; ततो हैव
विदाञ्चकार ब्रह्मेति ॥ १ ॥

sā brahmeti hovāca; brahmaṇo vā etad vijaye mahīyadhvam iti;
tato haiva vidāñcakāra brahmeti ॥ 1 ॥

She said, "It is *Brahman*. In the victory of *Brahman* indeed did you attain glory." Only thus Indra did know that it was *Brahman*.

The Ultimate Teaching

ALL the sciences attempt to find out truth in one way or another. The enquiry may either be from the side of material existence or from the mental side. In either case, what is sought for is the reality behind appearance. Whatever be its nature, where can it exist? It has to exist in and through the appearance. In other words, the Reality sought for does not exist apart from me, the enquirer, and also from the world I see around me. It cannot exist as an abstract entity. Just as the earth and the particles in it exist as non-different, the reality and appearance have to inhere in each other. The visualisation of the non-duality of appearance and reality is the ultimate aim of Vedānta.

Appearance Gains a New Dimension

What is seen before us as the world will be a big question mark until it is seen as a momentary unfoldment of the eternal Reality, like the *yakṣa* here. But when Reality is seen, the question is no longer a question. It disappears altogether, as the *yakṣa* did. What appears as the world and its observer, is the actualisation of the limitless creativity of the one Reality that always exists invisibly in what is visible. The *yakṣa* who appeared before the *deva*s represents the mysteriousness of the visible world. The invalidation of the dimension proper to the apparent world as having an existence of its own, and its gaining a new dimension as existing not apart from the one Reality, are represented by the disappearance of the *yakṣa* and the appearance of Umā who teaches the *deva*s.

Jñānins see the appearance of the world as not apart from the Existence (*sat*) of *Brahman*. Appearance thus gains an existential dimension in their vision. The *deva*s on seeing *yakṣa* (the mysterious universe), could not find out what it was. Umā taught them that what appeared as the world was nothing but *Brahman*. It was a little spark of its creativity that the *deva*s experienced as their victory, and what the *asura*s felt as their defeat. What was, and what is, always victorious is *Brahman* alone. Umā convinces Indra of this secret of *Brahmavidyā*. Thus, the allegorical narration of a revised version of a Purāṇic story, which was started at the beginning of the last section, ends with this *mantra*.

The Role of a Guru

Two types of seekers need the help of a guide. There are some who do not know the truth, but who are desirous of knowing it. But there are a few who know the truth, but do not know what they know is the truth. Both these types require help. But in the case of *Brahmavidyā*, this distinction is not relevant as the knowledge it deals with is a unique one. Even though what we see before us, including what we are, is nothing but the one Reality, we pass it for the world, and as a result find it as a source of all miseries. This illusory knowledge is what is called *avidyā* in Vedānta. To save the seeker from this illusion and to show that what always exists in every form is nothing but the reality of *Brahman*, is the role of a *guru*. This role was played exquisitely by Umā here.

Thus, the three *deva*s who had superiority only in the Vedic context, are accepted as superior in the higher level of Vedānta. This is an example of the revision of Vedism by Vedāntism. In the Vedas, the *deva*s are considered superior as they do favours to men. In Vedānta they become superior because it was they who knew *Brahman* first.

तस्माद् वा एते देवा अतितरामिवान्यान् देवान्, यदग्निर्वायुरिन्द्रस्ते
ह्येनन्नेदिष्ठं पस्पर्शुस्ते ह्येनत् प्रथमो विदाञ्चकार ब्रह्मेति ॥ २ ॥

tasmād vā ete devā atitarām ivānyān devān, yad agnir vāyur indras te hy enan nediṣṭhaṁ pasparśus te hy enat prathamo vidāñcakāra brahmeti ॥ 2 ॥

Therefore indeed these gods — Agni, Vāyu and Indra — are as if surpassing greatly the other gods. Because they indeed felt this *Brahman* closest. Because they firstly knew this as *Brahman*.

Social Status and its Basis

It has become a part of human life to assume a status to the state of life of an individual in the society. This could be on the basis of one's wealth, knowledge, caste, official positions, unselfish service, etc. Even the colour of the skin sometimes plays the role of a criterion for this superiority and inferiority. The superiority of one depends on the inferiority of another, based on some social prejudices and customs. These prejudices and customs by themselves are baseless. So they could generally be considered relativistic. Among these relative criteria, the most popular one is the wealth one accumulates and the luxurious amenities one has set. This is because money is the easiest thing that could be accumulated without any distinguishing mental qualities, and even adopting mean means. The worldly pleasures one could gather in such a manner could be supposed to have heaven as its apex.

Respectability of Wisdom

The denizens of heaven are the *deva*s. The *deva*s or gods of the Vedas, therefore, may be considered to represent the superior state of life in a relative and worldly sense. What men pray for, when propitiating gods by performing burnt sacrifices (*agnihotra*s), is also worldly pleasures here and hereafter. This heaven or *svarga* is referred to as immortal at the beginning of the *Kaṭha Upaniṣad*.[1] But this immortality belongs to the context of rituals. There is yet another kind of immortality which the same Upaniṣad declares later as its ultimate aim to be reached.

These two immortalities are referred to side by side in the *Kaṭha Upaniṣad* in order to enable the seeker to distinguish between the ultimate aims of rituals and wisdom. The heavenly pleasures attainable depend on the propitiatory rituals one performs in this life, which in turn depends on one's wealth and state of life. But the immortality attained by a *jñānin* does not depend on any such. It is self-founded (*ātma-niṣṭha*). It makes a *jñānin* or man of wisdom respectable to everyone.

The superiority of the *deva*s among living beings is based only on certain relative considerations. But the wisdom of the Upaniṣads is non-relative and absolute in nature. At the same time, this wisdom, or the Vedānta philosophy, has Vedism as its background. It was on the canvas of Vedism

1. *Kaṭha Upaniṣad*, I.i.13.

the philosophy of the Upaniṣads was painted. In this process, Vedānta had to give a new meaning, acceptable to its non-relative standpoint, to many of the Vedic concepts. Here the issue is the superiority of some *deva*s over the others, and also of Indra among the top ones.

The three *deva*s are considered here superior as they had direct contact with or experience of *Brahman*. They had this experience through Indra with the help of Umā. The ultimate Reality is experienced by a seeker as one's own Self. There is nothing nearer to one than one's own Self. Therefore it can be said to be the closest (*nediṣṭham*). The pity is that so close a reality is never seen by man. The three *deva*s became free of this pitiable state with the help of Umā and experienced the presence of *Brahman* as if feeling it (*pasparśuḥ*). The superiority attributed to the three *deva*s here need not be taken to be attainable only by some denizens of the other world. It is a superiority natural to all who directly experience the presence of *Brahman* in their life. There is no distinction between gods and men among the seekers. The *Taittirīya Upaniṣad* even says, all the gods carry offerings to the men who know *Brahman*.[2] Gods and men are equal there. Even among men, religion, caste, colour, nationality, sex or any other consideration has no place there.

तस्माद् वा इन्द्रोऽतितरामिवान्यान् देवान्; स ह्येनन्नेदिष्ठं पस्पर्श, स
ह्येनत् प्रथमो विदाञ्चकार ब्रह्मेति ॥ ३ ॥

tasmād vā indro 'titarām ivānyān devān; sa hy enan nediṣṭhaṁ
pasparśa, sa hy enat prathamo vidāñcakāra brahmeti ॥ 3 ॥

Therefore, indeed, Indra surpasses greatly, as it were, other gods. He indeed has come into close contact with this (*Brahman*). He indeed knew firstly that it (was) *Brahman*.

---

2. *Taittirīya Upaniṣad*, I.v.3.

Indra surpasses all the other gods for the same reason mentioned in the last *mantra*. Here Indra has a special status of being the one through whom Agni and Vāyu, and after them all other gods, knew *Brahman*.

The word *iva* (as it were) in the last and the present *mantras*, is to be noted. It indicates that the doctrine of the *Upaniṣad* proper is not concerned directly with the superiority of the gods, which is proper only to Vedism.

तस्यैष आदेशो यदेतद् विद्युतो व्यद्युतदा इतीन्न्यमीमिषदा इत्यधिदैव
तम् ॥ ४ ॥

tasyaiṣa ādeśo yad etad vidyuto vyadyutadā itīn nyamīmiṣadā
ity adhidaivatam ॥ 4 ॥

Of this *Brahman* there is this teaching: such a *Brahman* is, as it were, like the lightning that flashes forth, or like the winking of the eye. Thus is the teaching based on the experience of brightness.

The central problem of this Upaniṣad was presented in the first section, and it was answered in the best possible manner in the very same section. It was also made clear how *Brahman* is to be visualised as the causal Substance in all the manifested phenomena, not only physical but psychic and biological as well. It was shown in the second section, how this *Brahman* is to be known as a non-object, what the validity of such a knowledge is, and how this knowledge differs from ordinary knowledge. It was also shown that, in the real awareness of *Brahman*, one realises that, whatever appears to be the object of knowledge and also as subjective knowledge, is not different from that non-dual *Brahman*. The third section narrated a revised version of an episode of the Purāṇas, to substantiate what was taught in the former sections.

Another important issue is taken up now for consideration: how is that knowledge, which is known by those who do not know, and not known to those who do know, imparted to a seeker? The secret of wisdom is to be handed down by the process of imparting it to a seeking disciple by a *guru*. But the Truth to be imparted is of such a nature that it cannot be expressed in words. This is not a problem faced by a particular *guru* alone, but also by a disciple who wants to know: how is one to grasp it?

Brahmajñāna is not Merely an Ideation

An idea becomes fixed in our mind as the result of our logical thinking either connected with an event or otherwise. It could also be an imagery created by a fantasy. In either case, it assumes a definite form in our mind. Formulation of such an idea or imagery could be possible about *Brahman* also. All such ideations and fantasies are only functional modulations of an individual consciousness, which in turn is only a functional aspect of *Brahman*.

What is Adhyātma-jñāna?

When ideations, fantasies and such other mental imageries are understood as various functional modulations of the individual consciousness, it is called *adhyātma-jñāna*. Usually *adhyātma-jñāna* is understood as spiritual knowledge in a loose sense. But it has a definitive denotation. *Adhi* means, based on, and *ātma* means, oneself. Thus *adhyātma-jñāna* means, that knowledge which we formulate as a result of cogitations with oneself as the basic starting point. It could be called psychological knowledge, in the original sense of the term psyche. It will be shown in the next *mantra* how the knowledge of *Brahman* could be imparted from this standpoint. Another alternative is given in the present *mantra*. It is called *adhidaivata*.

What is Adhidaivata?

Sometimes something becomes revealed to us, as it were, by the explosion of a brightness from inside. It has a definitiveness of its own, but not as the conclusion of a logical reasoning. But, when logically examined, the revelation would be found undeniable. The ultimate Reality also becomes revealed to us as such an experience, while it remains a wonder. One such rarest experience is portrayed by Narayana Guru thus:

> Filled with word-content, that day
> the firmament shall blaze radiant,
> And in it shall become extinct all the
> visionary magic;
> Then too, that small voice completing
> tri-basic knowing
> Shall cease and Self-radiance prevail.[3]

One whose nature and content is brightness is called *deva* and *devatā* in Sanskrit. That which is related to *devatā* is *daivatam*. That kind of instruction which adopts Self-revelation as the basic standpoint is to be characterised as *adhidaivatam*. Self-revelation is an inner experience only, and hence it is not possible to impart it to another person in its completeness and vividness. So the help of two metaphors is relied on to say what it is.

Two Metaphors

The first metaphor is that of the lightning. The flash of a lightning in pitch darkness makes everything that was in the dark, evident all of a sudden. The words of great seers who had the direct experience of the ultimate Reality, affirm that their experience was also such a sudden flashing of inner brightness. Narayana Guru explains the inner details of such an experience thus:

---

3. *Ātmopadeśa Śatakam*, verse 52.

> Like the dawn altogether of ten thousand solar orbs
> Wisdom's function comes; such verily is that which tears
> Asunder this wisdom-hiding *māyā*-darkness here;
> And as the primal sun prevails.[4]

The tearing asunder of the *māyā*-darkness goes with the experiencing of the lightning referred to in the Upaniṣad here.

We start thinking of the ultimate meaning of life when we become doubtful about our own existence and about everything that we see around us. When the Truth is finally understood, we realise that it is one and the same Reality that manifests here as the world and also as "I" who observes It. It is this realisation that happens to one just like the flashing of lightning as referred to here in the Upaniṣad, and like the rising up of ten thousand suns altogether as mentioned by Narayana Guru. In the place of the concept that the world of multiplicity is the reality, one realises that it is the one Reality that appears here as the world. This certainty makes us well-founded in knowledge, which state is called that of a *sthita-prajña* in the *Bhagavad Gītā*.[5]

To such a person the Reality does not exist somewhere else. "I am *Brahman*" (*aham brahma asmi*) would never be mere words nor a mere idea for him. It is an actuality and reality directly experienced. Till that moment the Reality was, as it were, hidden in the pitch darkness of *māyā*.

The metaphor of lightning still does not give a complete picture of the experience meant here. The flashing of lightning lasts only for a moment, and everything goes back into obscurity again. But the Primal Sun that tears asunder the inner darkness never sets again. So a second metaphor is relied on to fulfil what is lacking in the first one.

---

4. Ibid., verse 35.
5. *Bhagavad Gītā*, II.55-72.

We don't see anything when our eyes are closed. Nothing but darkness exists then. But the entire world appears before us when the eyelid is opened. That experience continues to exist too. Similarly, in a state when our inner eye is closed due to ignorance, the Reality, even when existing before us, is not experienced. But, when the inner eye opens, the entire Reality becomes revealed. Then we don't see anything but Reality, and It never disappears again. The world, whose existence was felt to be mysterious, is realised to be nothing but the changeful self-expression of the changeless Reality. It continues to be so forever.

There is one more complementarity between these two metaphors. The experience of a flashing of lightning is caused by a stimulus from an external event. But the opening of the eyelid happens as a biological urge from within. The revelation of *Brahman* could neither be said to be caused by an internal urge nor by an external stimulation, because that Reality is neither inside nor outside, but both. It can never be put in words even in the form of a metaphor because there is no similar event in nature. So, to cross over this limitation of language, the *ṛṣi* of the Upaniṣad resorts to the method of referring to both the sides together and leaving the visioning of the non-duality in it to the contemplative seeker. This unusual method is common to almost all the scriptures.

अथाध्यात्मं यदेतद् गच्छतीव च मनोऽनेन चैतदुपस्मरत्यभीक्ष्णँ
सङ्कल्पः ॥ ५ ॥

athādhyātmaṁ yad etad gacchatīva ca mano 'nena caitad
upasmaraty abhīkṣṇaṁ saṅkalpaḥ ॥ 5 ॥

And now the teaching based on the individual consciousness. It is thus: that *Brahman* is the one towards which mind appears to move. By the same *Brahman*, as mind, it is remembered.

Repeated volition is also likewise.

The instruction on *Brahman* here is from the side of the individual consciousness. When we hear something, immediately an idea is formulated in the mind. Then we say, "I understand it." We always remember the object we understood, if we are interested in it. We always fancy many things about its usefulness. All these happen in an individual consciousness. But it has already been made clear that the Reality to be known with the help of the Upaniṣad is not an object of knowledge. In fact, *Brahman* Itself functions as the individual consciousness and tries to conceive it as an idea. That means, when our mind tries to think of *Brahman*, it is *Brahman* Itself that functions as the mind and its attempt to conceive it. The same is the case when we imagine, remember and have a volition to know, and so on.

तद्ध तद्वनं नाम तद्वनमित्युपासितव्यं; स य एतदेवं वेदाभिहैनँ सर्वाणि
भूतानि संवाञ्छन्ति ॥ ६ ॥

taddha tadvanaṁ nāma tadvanam ity upāsitavyaṁ; sa ya etad
evaṁ vedābhihainaṁ sarvāṇi bhūtāni saṁvāñchanti ॥ 6 ॥

That (*Brahman*) verily is called the dearest of all. It is worshippable as the dearest of all. Whosoever knows it thus, him, all beings seek for solace.

The Worshippable Aspect of Brahman

Two methods of instruction regarding the non-dual *Brahman* were shown in the two preceding *mantras*, one as a sudden revelation of brightness and the other as an individual's concept. These two are indications from two opposite poles, concerning an inexpressible Truth.

When the indescribable Reality is seen thus, as if having two describable facets, it could be considered as "the dearest of all" (*tadvanam*). The word *tadvanam* means "that *vanam*". *Vanam* means that which could be enjoyed or appreciated (*vana sambhajane*). The indescribable *Brahman*, when expressed by way of instruction, is not only the dearest, it becomes worshippable too.

We saw at the beginning of this Upaniṣad that *Brahman* would never be something worshippable and it was repeatedly asserted. It is in the light of that assertion we have to see the statement here that it is worshippable as *tadvanam*. That means, the non-worshippable *Brahman* is purely non-dual, while the same when visualised as instructible, as having two describable facets, becomes adorable. The process of adoration has to be a mutual cancelling out of these facets to result in the very same non-dual *Brahman*.

The Two-sided Instruction

A real *jñānin* is aware of the indescribability of the Reality. But his wisdom becomes useless to anyone else if he remains silent in the bliss of his experience. There are very rare *jñānins* who feel an internal agony in their attempt to share with others somehow the beatitude they are experiencing. Seekers would look at him hopefully, and would approach him entreating for wisdom.

The kind-hearted *jñānin* knows that the Reality he knows cannot be taught to others as such. So he resorts to describing how it could be seen from different viewpoints. What we find in the Upaniṣads by way of instructions are such visualisations. Showing it from two opposing standpoints enables the seekers to find the Reality for themselves by cancelling out the oppositeness of visions. The *adhidaivata* and *adhyātma* views presented in the preceding *mantras* were of such a nature. There could be many such opposing viewpoints which would be equally valid. Such dual and opposite ways of approach, and their mutual cancelling out in contemplation, are more vividly put forth by Narayana Guru thus:

> The atom and the infinite, as also being and non-being,
> Both from either side do shine forth; this experience too
> Of being as well as non-being thereafter becomes extinct,
> And devoid of foundation, forever, both cease to be.
>
> Within the glory of wisdom, the atom bereft of parts becomes extinct,
> And the infinite too, that day attains perfection;
> Without directly experiencing, this cannot be known — this boundless
> Stuff of pure intelligence, this silence-filled ocean of immortal Bliss![6]

The duality of the immanent and the transcendent of Immanuel Kant belongs to the same context. Mind-matter, here-hereafter, microcosm-macrocosm, being-non-being, existence-non-existence, subject-object, are all similar dualities. Instruction is possible from all these dual standpoints.

Those *jñānin*s who resort to these dual aspects of teaching always take care not to lean toward or be prejudiced by either, and to keep always in a neutrality, as clearly indicated in the words of Narayana Guru quoted above.

Such *jñānin*s are to be called *guru*s. Their peacefulness and unlimited generosity attract those who are caught in the feverishness of life. They look hopefully at them for succour. They take refuge in them and submit before them all their weariness, hopeful of relief. Such *guru*s or Masters are always the refuge of the sufferers. So it is said here, "Him, all beings seek for solace."

---

6. *Ātmopadeśa Śatakam*, 96, 97.

उपनिषदं भो ब्रूहीत्युक्ता त उपनिषद् ब्राह्मीं वाव त
उपनिषदमब्रूमेति ॥ ७ ॥

upaniṣadaṁ bho brūhītyuktā ta upaniṣad brāhmīṁ vāva ta
upaniṣadam abrūmeti ॥ 7 ॥

The disciple again says: "O Master, teach me the secret wisdom." The Master replies: "The secret wisdom has been taught to you. We have taught you the secret of *Brahman* indeed."

Why the Same Question is Repeated

Whatever is to be given by way of instruction, and whatever is possible by way of instruction, regarding *Brahmavidyā* has been explained to the disciple by the last *mantra*. Why does the disciple ask again: "O Master, teach me the secret wisdom."

It was made clear, as part of the instruction, that this secret will not confine itself to be the meaning of any word. There is thus chance for the disciple not to notice the termination of the instruction, which was only through words. It may tempt him to ask the above question.

The listener might not have become satisfied even after hearing the last word that could be given, for what is to be understood is something beyond words. So, in his impatience, the student might have been tempted to ask again, "Please tell me the secret."

In the context of the *Kena Upaniṣad*, even such a possibility seems out of place. We saw in the second section that the *guru* made it clear to the disciple that the wisdom of the Upaniṣad was of such a nature that it was known to those who do not know, and unknown to those who know. After hearing these words, the disciple contemplated on it for a long time, and then came back and reacted to the *guru* saying, "I do not think that I know it well. Nor do I think that I do not know it." From this statement of the disciple it is to be guessed that he understood what the *guru* intended.

We are the Questioners

This Upaniṣad is really not meant for that particular disciple or any other disciple like him, but it is meant for us. We are not so intuitive in our approach, nor do we have that mental stamina the disciple of the Upaniṣad had. What we try to do therefore would be to grasp the secret of the wisdom from the words of the Upaniṣad.

Even after searching through the entire text we may find ourselves at a loss. We therefore feel, what we wanted to know was not yet disclosed to us. So we ask ourselves, "Where is the answer I was seeking for?" We turn to the teacher and ask him, "Please teach me the secret." This question of ours is merely put by the *ṛṣi* of the Upaniṣad in the guise of that of the disciple.

Our Conditioned Mind

Our mind is so conditioned that we become satisfied only on getting a direct answer to a question. The two main questions asked in *Brahmavidyā* are, "Who am I?" and "From where did this world come?" When we ask, "Who am I?," it implies that I exist unquestionably. Similarly, when we ask, "From where did this world come?" we accept as a basic premise that this world exists. But the teaching given in the Upaniṣad is that neither "I" nor this world has an existence of its own. There is only one Reality that exists. It is that Reality that appears as "I" as well as the world. The answer we get to the questions we asked is that, ultimately neither I nor the world exists. This answer might seem very vague to us in the beginning.

No Direct Answer Possible

Instead of giving a direct answer to the question, the *guru* of the Upaniṣad shows the questioner that the basic premise on which the questions were based was wrong.

When we ask a question, we neither know that there is a basic premise in it nor that, that premise could be a questionable one. We therefore expect a direct answer. So long as we don't understand what is basically wrong in our question, we shall continue to feel that the *guru* did not give the final answer. So we ask him again to teach the secret of wisdom.

We feel satisfied if we get an answer like, "The world came down here from the empty space" or "The world came out of atoms" or even "The world was created by God." But the answer given in the Upaniṣad is not of that kind.

The *Kaṭha Upaniṣad* expounds *Brahmavidyā* as an answer to the question, "What happens to the soul after death?" This is an unanswerable question that wells up in the minds of everyone. Had the answer been like, "The soul of the dead will go to *Vaikuṇṭha*, the *devaloka* (the world of gods), the *pitṛloka* (the world of manes), the hell, or even to some other womb to be reborn," we would have felt that we got an answer. We don't care for the tenability of any of them. At the same time, we find it very difficult to understand the real teaching of the Upaniṣad, that the Self has no birth and death and that it is the only Reality.

No Private Teaching

Even after studying the entire *Kaṭha Upaniṣad* a student might ask, "Where does the soul of the dead go?" The answer that there is no other answer than the one given in the *Kaṭha Upaniṣad* would not satisfy the questioner. His or her immediate reaction could be, "That is all right. That I know. But this is for my private understanding." The only answer that can be given to such a question is, "My friend, go and do *tapas*. This question will then disappear." The *guru* of the *Kena Upaniṣad* also does the same in the next *mantra*.

The question was caused by the incompetence of the questioner to know the full import of the teaching of the Upaniṣad. This competence is not something that could be taught. It is one's own intense yearning and self-imposed discipline in life that make one competent for this wisdom.

तस्यै तपो दमः कर्मेति प्रतिष्ठा वेदाः सर्वाङ्गानि सत्यमायतनम् ॥ ८ ॥

tasyai tapo damaḥ karmeti pratiṣṭhā vedāḥ sarvāṅgāni satyaṁ āyatanam ॥ 8 ॥

Austerity, self-control and action are its support. Scriptures constitue all limbs. Truth is its abode.

All the Upaniṣads are meant to teach *Brahmavidyā* (the Science of the Absolute). But no one seems to have become a knower of *Brahman* (*brahma-jñānin*) merely by learning the Upaniṣads.

The Upaniṣads are the words of the knowers of *Brahman*, but some prerequisites on our part are essential in order that the secret hidden in these words become well rooted in us. Austerity (*tapas*), self-control (*dama*) and action (*karma*) are the qualities mentioned here as the prerequisites. These are the bases on which this wisdom is to be well founded.

Tapas (Austerity)

A study of the biographies of great seers and men of wisdom reveals that it was not by mere studying of scriptures, but by an intense search accompanied by a kind of heating up of the self that they attained the goal. This self-heating is called *tapas*. The word literally means heating up.

Some Upaniṣads pointedly state that *tapas* is the means for attaining the knowledge of *Brahman*. For example, the *Taittirīya Upaniṣad* says, "Through austerity seek to know

Brahman."[7] The place of *tapas* in the attainment of wisdom has been emphasised in different contexts of various Upaniṣads.

Tapas is not something on which any instruction can be given. It is a process of heating up that happens in the psyche of the seeker. Metals become pure when heated up. Likewise, when the seeker directs himself on to the path of searching for Reality with an intense effort, it happens to be a process of inner heating up. Nataraja Guru explains the implications of *tapas* thus:

> Contemplation implies a form of ascent through intensity of thought, as it were, under high pressure. Passive and lukewarm attitudes are not conducive to yield the results of true contemplation, where the inertia, the aches and pains of the body, or even love of easy-chair comfort are to be left behind by the aspirant. There is a factor called *tapas* (burning up) which presupposes an agony of some sort, and implies intensity of research, full alertness, supported by clear memory, willingness to give full attention to the subject or problem at hand, and power to listen or will to believe on a basis, or correct speculation which balances belief. Such are some of the known prerequisites here.[8]

All our bodily, verbal and mental activities become spontaneously so regulated as to be conducive to the final goal in this intense effort. The *Bhagavad Gītā* therefore in chapter XVIII mentions three kinds of *tapas*, namely, bodily (*śārīrīkam*), verbal (*vāṅmayam*) and mental (*mānasam*). A piece of metal when heated up, first becomes red hot and then becomes white hot. Finally it melts and burns up where no metal would be visible. What is seen would be a radiance of brightness alone. The same happens in the case of self-heating also. When its

---

7. *tapasā brahma vijijñāsasva* — *Taittirīya Upaniṣad*, III.1-5.

8. Nataraja Guru, *The Philosophy of a Guru*, p. 28, Narayana Gurukula, Varkala, India, 1986.

intensity turns the self (oneself) into an experience of pure effulgence, the Reality sought for and the effort made to attain it would be found to be non-different. That is why in the *Taittirīya Upaniṣad*, along with the words "Through austerity seek to know *Brahman*" it is said, "Austerity is *Brahman*."[9] That is where *tapas* (austerity) becomes the real basis on which *Brahmavidyā* is founded, as indicated in the present *mantra*.

Dama (Self-restraint)

The true seekers who lead an austere life could often be seen as withdrawn from the society, finding their abode in some solitude. They even choose caves in mountain ranges as their dwellings. Thus, those who go to the caves in mountains to do spiritual practices are often called *tapasvins* (practitioners of austerity), at least in India. But mere living in a cave does not make one a *tapasvin*. The real seekers go to the caves only to save themselves from the distractions of the society. This desire to keep away from worldly attractions is called *dama* (self-restraint).

It won't be wrong to say that the *dama* referred to here implies all the six qualities considered essential prerequisites for a seeker. They are *śama* (calmness), *dama* (self-restraint), *uparati* (self-withdrawal), *titikṣa* (forbearance), *śraddhā* (faith), and *samādhāna* (self-settledness). All these are certain regulations one adopts in life, which are conducive to the attainment of the goal of the seekers, and a part of the behaviour pattern of the one who has reached the goal. The *tapas* and *dama* here are like the two legs for men to walk. In the spiritual progression of the seeker, these lead him forward, mutually balancing each other.

---

9. *tapo brahmeti* — *Taittirīya Upaniṣad*, III.1-5.

Karma (Action)

Such a progression is a creative one. The seeker may outwardly appear to be leading an idle life, but his inner life will be extremely creative. This creative power is not his own. It is only part of the creativity of the entire nature. Even a minute particle in nature is endowed with a creativity of its own. In the case of a seeker who leads an austere life, he makes use of this creative power to find out the depths of the same creative nature. That is the action (*karma*) that goes on in him. In other words, it is the creativity or power for action in an individual that makes use of *tapas* and *dama* as tools for finding out the secret of the creativity of nature. Thus, *karma* or action also becomes, along with *tapas* and *dama*, a support in attaining the secret wisdom of the Upaniṣad.

Scriptures

All the Upaniṣads are pictorial representations of certain visions of one or more *ṛṣis* (seers). We could also say that Upaniṣads are the concretised forms of the wisdom-secret. Strictly speaking, Upaniṣads do not form part of the Vedas. They are only appended to them at their end. But in principle Upaniṣads are to be considered as Vedas, for the word Veda means "knowledge." In India, the word *veda* is used only as referring to the four compendia of hymns, called *Ṛgveda*, *Yajurveda*, *Sāmaveda* and *Atharvaveda*. But in a universal sense, all the scriptures of the world are to be considered as Vedas. Any scripture that reveals the secret wisdom is a Veda. All the scriptures of the world are concretised forms of one and the same wisdom. The concretisation of something abstract can take place in various ways and forms. The same is the case with the secret wisdom also. All such formulations of this wisdom deserve the title Veda.

Thus we could say, all the scriptures constitute the body or limbs of the secret wisdom of the Upaniṣads. Bādarāyaṇa, in the *Brahmasūtras*, says all the scriptures have the ultimate Reality as their source.[10] The same could also be brought in here for contemplation to see how suggestive are the words, *vedāḥ sarvāṅgāṇi* (scriptures constitute all its limbs).

Satyam (Truth)

Because of the abstractness of the experiential positive context of the Truth understood here, we are likely to fall into the error of thinking that Truth has nothing to do with actual life. Our enquiry began from the actuality of the world. The entire teaching becomes meaningless and valueless if that actuality is denied.

Though the enquiry was begun from the actuality of the world, the Truth we attained seems completely alien to it. We may therefore doubt whether the wisdom we gained is regarding this world. So we might again want to know the Truth.

To save us from this, it is necessary to see the positive experiential content of Truth as the existential content also. In other words, existentiality has to be made the abode of the experiential awareness. It is then that this Reality becomes *sat, cit* and *ānanda* at the same time. That is why it is said here, "Truth is its abode" (*satyam āyatanam*). One finds one's actual existence not different from the one absolute Existence.

यो वा एतामेवं वेदापहत्य पाप्मानमनन्ते स्वर्गे लोके ज्येये प्रतितिष्ठति
प्रतितिष्ठति ॥ ९ ॥

yo vā etām evaṁ vedāpahatya pāpmānam anante svarge loke
jyeye pratitiṣṭhati pratitiṣṭhati ॥ 9 ॥

Whoever knows this (*Brahmavidyā*) thus, he, overcoming sin,

10. *śāstra-yonitvāt* — *Brahmasūtras*, I.i.2.

becomes firmly established in the endless and supreme world of heaven; yes, he becomes firmly established.

This last stanza is in the form of an envoy. The benefit of knowing the secret hidden in the Upaniṣad is, one becoming well established in the endless supreme world of heaven, overcoming all the sufferings.

The *svarga* or heaven is a Vedic concept. It is a world that can be reached by doing meritorious deeds (*puṇya-karmas*). But the enjoyment in that heaven is not endless (*ananta*). When the merit gained runs out, one has to come back to this world again. That means, the happiness attainable by Vedism is not an absolute one.

But the ultimate goal of the Upaniṣads is absolute Happiness (*ānanda*) which is endless and beyond all the merits and demerits (*puṇya* and *pāpa*).

Though the word "heaven" is used here, being faithful to its Vedic background, it is a heaven that is endless (*ananta*) and supreme (*jyeya*). It is not different from the state of final release and the immortality mentioned earlier. Such is the attainment promised by the Upaniṣad.

ओं आप्यायन्तु ममाङ्गानि वाक् प्राणश्चक्षुः श्रोत्रमथो बलमिन्द्रियाणि च सर्वाणि। सर्वं ब्रह्मौपनिषदं माऽहं ब्रह्म निराकुर्यां मा मा ब्रह्म निराकरोदनिराकरणमस्त्वनिराकरणं मेऽस्तु। तदात्मनि निरते य उपनिषत्सु धर्मास्ते मयि सन्तु ते मयि सन्तु॥

ओं शान्तिः शान्तिः शान्तिः।

auṁ āpyāyantu mamāṅgāni vāk prāṇaścakṣuḥ śrotram atho balam indriyāṇi ca sarvāṇi | *sarvaṁ brahmaupaniṣadaṁ mā 'ham brahma nirākuryāṁ mā mā brahma nirākarodanirākaraṇam astvanirākaraṇaṁ me astu* | *tad ātmani nirate ya upaniṣatsu dharmās te mayi santu te mayi santu* ||

auṁ śāntiḥ śāntiḥ śāntiḥ |

May my limbs, speech, vital breath, eyes, ears, as also my strength and all the senses grow vigorous. All this is the Absolute (*Brahman*) referred to in the Upaniṣads. May I never negate the Absolute. May the Absolute never negate me. May there be no negating. May there be non-negating in me. Let those basic tenets enunciated in the Upaniṣads, rest in the Self. Let them be in me. Aum Peace! Peace! Peace!

Glossary

Abhayam: Fearlessness. One of the aspects in which the knowledge of *Brahman* is experienced as a value.

Acit: The opposite of *cit*. Denotes physical matter in the philosophy of Rāmānuja.

Ādhibhautika-duḥkha: Sufferings caused by other beings.

Adhidaiva: The way of looking at reality with the universal effulgent aspect of it as the reference point. (from *adhi* — to have a basis, and *daiva* — that which is related to brightness).

Ādhidaivika-duḥkha: Sufferings caused by providence.

Adhikaraṇa: A section or context dealing with a particular topic. According to the Mīmāṁsakas an *adhikaraṇa* has five elements, namely *viṣaya*, the subject matter to be explained; *saṁśaya*, the doubt or question that arises upon that matter; *pūrvapakṣa*, the anterior critique which questions the argument; *uttara-pakṣa* or *siddhānta-pakṣa*, the answer or demonstrated conclusion; and *saṅgati*, pertinency or relevance.

Advaita: Non-duality. The finally attained unitive vision, when the vestiges of every shade of duality, such as one and the many, particular and universal, psychological and cosmological, have all been transcended by a man of philosophical vision.

Agni-hotra: The burnt offering or fire-sacrifice enjoined by the Vedas.

Aham brahmāsmi: See *Mahā-vākyas*.

Ajñānin: The ignorant. The opposite of *jñānin*.

Ākāśa: Space. That which gives room for everything to exist. Also called *vyoman*.

Amṛta: Immortality or the immortal Reality. Poetically imagined as the elixir in a golden pot that emerged from the Milk-Ocean as a result of churning it by *deva*s and *asura*s together.

Ānanda: Bliss.To be understood in the context of the Good in Western philosophy as a supreme value. *Sat, Cit, Ānanda* are terms conjointly used to describe the Absolute (*Brahman*) in Vedānta. Concerning an individual being, it is to be understood as the value consciousness that enables one to evaluate his own experiences either as pleasant or unpleasant.

Antarmukha-anveṣaṇa: Interiorised enquiry for Reality.

Apara: See *para*.

Aparokṣa anubhūti: Literally immediate experience. The intuitive experience of one's own identity with the absolute Reality or *Brahman*. The satisfaction of fulfilment of enquiry on one's finding the Reality searched for as oneself.

Aṛivu: A Malayalam word signifying consciousness. Often used as a synonym of the Self by Narayana Guru, in the sense of pure Consciousness whose functional aspects are experienced as various mental faculties. As the Ultimate Reality it is boundless.

Arthavāda: The exegesis of Vedas. Discussion of meaning, as opposed to *vidhi* which implies ritualist injunctions.

Asuras: The opposite of *suras* or *devas* (gods — the fair or bright entities inhabiting the Vedic heaven). Demons. This idea might have come into being with reference to anyone who opposed the Āryan penetration ideologically or in historical activity. The conflict between the *devas* and *asuras* permeates the whole of the spiritual literature of the Vedic Indians and has to be understood historically or in pure dialectics according to the requirements of the context. Max-Müller thinks there is an affinity between *Ahura* (*Ahurea Mazda*) of the Zoroastrians and *Asura*.

Ātman (*Ātma*): The self (from the root *āt*, to pervade). The invisible reality or stuff that pervades any visible form. Often confused with *jīva* (the soul). Used in slightly altered senses according to contexts. The simplest meaning of the word is "I" or "oneself."

Avidyā: Nescience or ignorance. That because of which one takes the unreal as the Real and the Real as the unreal. The root cause of all sufferings.

Avyakta: That which is not specific and definable. The opposite of *vyakta*.

Bhagavad Gītā: Part of the *Mahābhārata* (an epic of India) consisting of eighteen chapters, in which Kṛṣṇa as Guru instructs Arjuna, the secrets of the mysterious science of contemplation called *Brahmavidyā* and *Yogaśāstra*. It contains the quintessence of all the Upaniṣads.

Bhakti: The devotional type of religious life in which emotions have a large place.

Biṁba pratibiṁba bhāva: The notion that a soul is a reflected image of God.

Brahmajñāna: The knowledge of the Absolute.

Brahman: The Absolute. Literally, that which is always growing.

Brahmasūtras: Original aphorisms of canonical rank on Vedānta. The book sometimes called the *Vedānta Sūtras*, is attributed to Bādarāyaṇa, sometimes identified with Vyāsa or Vedavyāsa. Its importance is enhanced as Śaṅkara commented upon it, as also Madhva and Rāmānuja. Their study thus gives a thorough grounding for a student on Vedānta in its anterior and posterior forms as restated by Śaṅkara. (See *Prasthāna-traya*).

Brahmavidyā: The science of *Brahman* or the Absolute. Another name of Vedānta.

Buddhi: Intellect, knowledge.

Cit: Literally, "consciousness." The all-pervading imperishble Reality in all the perishable forms. Its existence is as pure consciousness. Hence *Brahman* is designated as *Cit*. See *Sat* and *Ānanda* also.

Darśana: Literally, "vision." The Indian equivalent to "philosophy." Vision of Reality as seen from the point of view of a given system of philosophy. Nyāya, Vaiśeṣika, Sāṁkhya, Yoga, Pūrva-Mīmāṁsā and Uttara-Mīmāṁsā are the six such systems of Indian philosophy. Narayana Guru, in his *Darśanamālā*, uses this word to mean any particular point of view of the non-dual Reality. He presents ten such visions strung together systematically into a garland.

Darśana Mālā: One of the major philosophical compositions of the Guru Narayana in Sanskrit. Literally, "The Garland of Visions." It consists of ten chapters of ten verses each. Each chapter is a vision of the Absolute from a particular philosophical perspective. All the ten visions are strung together in the invisible thread of advaita or non-duality.

Devaloka: The world of gods, heaven.

Devatā: A deity. A god as understood in the context of adoration or worship. Every Vedic hymn has a deity who is praised, a *chandas*, a particular metre in which it is composed, and a *ṛṣi*, the seer who composed it.

Dharma: (From *dhṛ* — to support). The system supporting the cosmos. An individual's behaviour pattern in tune with the cosmic system. Such a pattern of life is to be called righteous life.

Dhīra: Brave, bold, courageous. Etymologically, "one who imparts knowledge."

Dvaita: Duality or dualism. The popular name of Madhva's philosphy. This name is given deridingly to the Madhva system by other schools. He calls his philosophy *tattva-vāda* (the doctrine of the ultimate principle).

Guru: (From *gu* — darkness, and *ru* — counteract). The banisher of darkness or ignorance. A spiritual teacher or preceptor.

Indra: The first of the gods of the Vedic heaven with Mithra, Varuṇa and other presiding deities of phenomenal aspects. Indra's heaven is where all desires are fulfilled, and where plenty prevails.

Jaḍa: Inert matter.

Jīva: The Sanskrit equivalent to soul. Often confused with *ātman*, the self. Literally, that which sustains through breathing (*jīva-prāṇadhāraṇe*). To be precise, it is the Sanskrit equivalent to the biological term "living organism."

Jivanmukta: One who attains final release while living.

Jñāna: Wisdom. Wisdom concerning the ultimate Reality.

Jñānin: One who possesses *jñāna*. One who has attained enlightenment. *Jñāna* means Wisdom as contrasted with *karma* (works or rituals). *Jñāna-mārga* or the way of Wisdom gives primacy to reason and intuition.

Kaiṁkarya: Service to God.

Kāma: The Eros of India. Rati is his consort. The central eye of Śiva, that erupts fire, is said to have burnt Kāma to ashes when Kāma aimed his flowery-arrow at Śiva, in order to make him erotic, as commissioned by the gods who needed a martial deity. The war-god was born of Pārvatī, however, in circumstances portrayed by Kālidāsa in his epic poem called *Kumāra-sambhava* (The Birth of the War-God).

Kāraṇa: The cause. Gold is the cause and ornament is the effect. What really exists is gold alone. Similarly, what really exists in the world is *Brahman* alone, which is its cause. This way of thinking is called *sat-kāraṇa-vāda* (argument giving primacy to cause).

Karma: Action. All actions are connoted by this term, more especially ritualistic actions.

Kṣatriya: The warrior class. One of the four classes of the Indian caste-system. Originally refers to the psychological type which has prowess, brightness, firmness, skill, generosity, dignity and never-absconding as its main characteristics.

Madhva: Founder of the dualist school of Vedānta.

Mahā-vākyas: Literally, the great sentences. Applied to the conclusive formula of Vedāntic wisdom, such as *tat tvam asi* (that art thou), *aham brahmāsmi* (I am *Brahman*), *prajñānam brahma* (consciousness is *Brahman*), *ayam ātmā brahma* (this Self is *Brahman*), *auṁ tat sat* (auṁ that is what is real), *sarvam-khalvidam brahma* (everything here is *brahman* indeed).

Mahimā: Greatness. Etymologically, "the quality of being worshippable."

Manana: See *Nididhyāsana*.

Manas: Mind. That which is constituted of *manas* is called *manomaya*. *Manas* consists of the questioning and imagining faculties of consciousness.

Māyā: The mysterious urge inherent in the Absolute (*Brahman* or *ātman*) to unfold itself as all the worlds and the phenomenon of life. The very appearing of the world caused thus ends up in becoming a sort of veil put over the Absolute, hiding its vision from our view and making the illusion that the apparent world is the real.

Nārada: A dubious sort of holy figure or *ṛṣi* who moves between the *devas* and men and used perhaps in Indian literature whenever the Āryan and pre-Āryan sets of spiritual values had to be related through the aid of literary devices. He is a tale-bearer, reporting the vicious and virtuous, and recommending appropriate reward and punishment. Nārada is the reputed author of the *Bhaktisūtras* or Aphorisms of Devotion, and he carries a stringed instrument as he moves from one plane of existence to another. He is more Vedic than pre-Vedic.

Nididhyāsana: The last stage of gaining wisdom. *Śravaṇa* (hearing the word of instruction from the *guru*) and *manana* (intense cogitation on what is heard from the *guru*) are the two stages preceding.

Pāpa: Sin acquired through evil deeds.

Parā: Beyond, pertaining to the ultimate or supreme as opposed to the immanent here and now aspect of reality which is *aparā*. It could mean, "the transcendent."

Pāramārthika: This is contrasted with *vyāvahārika*. The pure, rational or idealist aspect of life which has little or nothing to do with social or other obligations or necessities (*parama* — ultimate; and *arthika* — as the aim).

Paratantra: The state of being dependent on someone or something else.

Pārvatī: The consort or *śakti* aspect of Śiva. She is the daughter of the Himālayas and is also a huntress, and known under various aspects in mythology and iconography.

Pitṛloka: The world of the departed souls, (from *pitṛ* — manes or departed souls, and *loka* — the world).

Prakṛti: Nature. Literally, that which is always in an active state. This activeness is inherent in the ultimate Reality or *Brahman*. *Brahman* in an active state is called *prakṛti*.

Prasthāna-traya: Common name to denote the three basic textbooks of Vedānta, namely The Upaniṣads, The *Brahmasūtras* and The *Bhagavad Gītā*.

Pralaya: The deluge. Literally, proper dissolution.

Pravacana: Discourse given by a learned person or *guru*. After completing formal education under a *guru*, a student has to continue his studies at home through self-study (*svādhyāya*) complemented by attending discourses of the learned as and when occasion arises. Finally, he would have to give *pravacana*s himself.

Puṇya: Merits acquired through good deeds.

Purāṇa: Literally, "the ancient." The collection of legends of antiquity. Meant mainly for teaching laymen the philosophy of the Upaniṣads with the help of numerous tales.

Puruṣa: Literally, "Person." The word is used both in the universal and particular senses. In the universal sense He is the cosmic person who has the entire cosmos for His body. In this sense He is often called *virāṭpuruṣa*.

Rāmānuja: Founder of the *Viśiṣṭādvaita* school of Vedānta.

Ṛg-Veda: See *Vedas*.

Sādhanā: The spiritual discipline undergone for the attainment of a particular goal (*siddhi*).

Śākteya: Those who follow the cult of Śakti-worship.

Śakti: See Pārvatī.

Śama: Checking and turning away of the mind from its distractions, one of the six qualities to be developed by self-effort as part of the spiritual discipline. The other five are *dama* (restraining the senses), *uparati* (non-dependence on the external), *titikṣā* (endurance), *śraddhā* (full faith in the words of one's *guru* and of the scriptures) and *samādhāna* (to have the thought of *Brahman* always in mind).

Sāma-Veda: See *Vedas*.

Saṁhāra: The disssolution of the world.

Sāṁkhya: One of the six systems of Indian philosophy. The other five are *Nyāya, Vaiśeṣika, Yoga, Pūrva Mīmāṁsā* and *Uttara Mīmāṁsā*. The last one is also known as Vedānta.

Śaṅkara: The founder of the non-dualistic (*Advaita*) school of Vedānta.

Śāntipāṭha: Peace invocation with which an Upaniṣad begins.

Śarīra: Literally, "that which perishes." The physical body or the visible form.

Sat: That which exists always. The subsisting reality in all the transient forms of the visible world, even as gold is the subsisting reality in all ornaments. *Brahman* as this subsisting Reality is designated as *sat*. See *ānanda* and *cit* also.

Satyam: Truth or Reality, metaphysically understood.

Śiva: The ancient hero-god from the times of prehistory, associated with radical virility and renunciation. He is an unconventional god like Dionysos, wearing skins and dancing in ecstasy, drunk with cosmic consciousness. He is the most ancient and the most important figure of the Indian pantheon, and occupies his seat in Benares in the plains and Kailāsa in the Himālayas.

Sphoṭa: The name of the Indian theory of semantics. Literally, "bursting out." A meaning bursts out in the mind just on hearing the utterance of a word.

Śraddhā: Belief in the veracity of one's *guru*'s words and also in the teachings of the basic scriptures.

Śravaṇa: See *Nididhyāsana*.

Sṛṣṭi: Creation. Literally, "surging up." What is called creation is merely the emergence of a new form in what already exists.

Sthitaprajña: One who is fully stabilised in inner awareness.

Sthiti: The existence of the created world.

Svādhyāya: The self-study a student has to continue at home after completing formal education under a *guru* and leaving the *gurukula*.

Svarga: The Vedic heaven or paradise, inhabited by *deva*s (gods) whose chief is Indra.

Svatantra: The state of being independent.

Tapas: Austere self-discipline. Literally, "heating up."

Umā: One of the *śakti* aspects of Śiva, as the beautiful and radiant daughter of the Himālayas, portrayed in Kālidāsa's *Kumāra-sambhava* and in the *Kena Upaniṣad* (III.12) (See Pārvatī).

Upaniṣad: Wisdom texts appended to the Vedas. Also called Vedānta as it appears at the end of the Vedas, and *jñānakāṇḍa* as it deals with wisdom. The word literally means, "to sit nearby and below" (*Upa* = just below, *ni* = nearby, *ṣat* = to sit down). The name indicates a disciple sitting beside a *guru*. The word also means "the secret teaching." The Upaniṣads teach the philosophy of *Brahman*, the Absolute. The ten major Upaniṣads are *Īśa, Kena, Kaṭha, Praśna, Muṇḍaka, Māṇḍūkya, Taittirīya, Aitareya, Chāndogya* and *Bṛhadāraṇyaka*.

Uparati: Cessation of desire-motivation especially when it applies to merit in the ritualistic sense of the Vedas.

Upāsanā: Worshipping a deity.

Vaikuṇṭha: The abode of Viṣṇu. Literally, "where there is no dullness."

Varṇa: Literally, "colour." Misinterpreted as caste distinction. According to the *Bhagavad Gītā*, the four psychological types or colouration, natural with human beings.

Vedānta: When the Vedic teachings had been revalued in philosophical terms by later *ṛṣis* (sages), a body of literature called *Vedānta* arose in the history of Indian thought. These often go contrary to the Vedic tendencies of rituals and obligations, announcing freedom and stressing Self-realisation. Later we find Śaṅkara, Rāmānuja and Madhva referred to as three typical Vedāntic philosophers although the *guru*s of the Vedāntic line (*paramparā*) are many. (See also *Upaniṣad*).

Vedas: The early Sanskrit writings in praise of Indra, Varuṇa and other phenomenal gods of nature; later overshadowed by the philosophical concept of the Absolute or *Brahman* in the Upaniṣads. The four chief *Veda*s are *Ṛg*, *Sāma*, *Yajus* and *Atharva*.

Vidyā: Knowledge. That because of which one understands the Real as the Real and the unreal as the unreal.

Vijñāna: Any specific or applied form of knowledge or wisdom.

Viśiṣṭādvaita: The qualified non-dualism of Rāmānuja. It considers the world and the numerous souls together as qualifying the Absolute or *Brahman* forming Its or His body.

Viṣṇu: The second of the Hindu trinity, of which Brahmā, the creator is the first and Maheśvara or Śiva is the last. Śiva is also the destroyer. Viṣṇu is referred to as the preserver, although taken by themselves each of them is in turn preserver and destroyer. These result from the fusing of three cosmological and psychological currents of religious thought in India.

Vyakta: That which is specific and definable.

Vyoman: See *Ākāśa*.

Yājñavalkya: A *ṛṣi*. The most important teacher of the *Bṛhadāraṇyaka Upaniṣad*.

Yakṣa: Literally, "a mysterious entity." A genie or mysterious apparition belonging to the series of angelic or awesome denizens of the spirit-world mentioned in Sanskrit literature, including, besides *Yakṣa*, the *Rākṣasa*, *Gandharva* and *Kinnara* as differing grades of beings.

Bibliography

Bergson, Henri, *Creative Evolution*, University Press of America, 1983.

———, *The Two Sources of Morality and Religion*, Indiana: University of Notre Dam Press, 1977.

Bhaskaran, Nair K., *Upaniṣad Deepti* (Malayalam), Trivandrum: K. Bhaskaran Nair, 1987.

Bhaskaran, Dr T., *Sree Nārāyaṇa Guruvinte Sampūrṇa Kr̥tikaḷ* (Malayalam) (Complete works of Sree Narayana Guru with Commentary), Calicut: Mathrubhoomi Publications, 1985.

Briggs, John P., *Looking Glass Universe*, New York: Corner Stone Library, 1984.

Chaṭṭampi Swami, *Nijānanda Vilāsam* (Malayalam), Varkala: Narayana Gurukula, 1980.

———, *Vedādhikāra Nirūpaṇam* (Malayalam), Kottayam: Rishiprasādam, 1986.

Capra, Fritjof, *The Tao of Physics*, Glasgow: Fantana Paperbacks, 1988.

Chakravarti, V.R. Srisaila, *The Philosophy of Sri Rāmānuja*, Madras: V.R.S. Chakravarti, 1974.

Dharmarāja Adhvarīndra, *Vedānta Paribhāṣā*, Sri Ramakrishna Math, Madras.

Hawking, Stephen W., *A Brief History of Time*, New York: Bantam Books, 1988.

Hofstadter, Douglas R., *The Mind's I*, New York: Bantam Books, 1982.

Hume, R.E., *The Thirteen Principal Upaniṣads*, Madras: Oxford University Press, 1965.

Keith, A.B., *The Religion and Philosophy of the Veda and Upaniṣads*, Delhi: Motilal Banarsidass, 1970.

Mahādeva Śāstri, Alladi, *The Taittirīya Upaniṣad*, Madras: Samata Books, 1980.

Mridananda Swami, *Taittirīyopaniṣad* (Commentary), Trichur: Sri Ramakrishna Ashram, 1976.

Murchie, Guy, *The Seven Mysteries of Life*, Boston: Houghton Mifflin Co., 1981.

Narayana Guru, Complete Works (Malayalam)., Varkala: Sivagiri Mutt, 1990.

Narayana Namboodiripād, O.M.C., *The Ṛg Veda* (Malayalam), Trichur: Kairali Press and Books, 1982.

Nataraja Guru, *An Integrated Science of the Absolute*, Varkala: Narayana Gurukula, 1977.

———, *The Bhagavad Gītā* — Commentary, Varkala: Narayana Gurukula, 1989.

———, *The Autobiography of An Absolutist*, Varkala: Narayana Gurukula, 1989.

———, *Life and Teachings of Narayana Guru*, Varkala: Narayana Gurukula, 1990.

———, *Dialectical Methodology*, Varkala: Narayana Gurukula, 1973.

———, *Wisdom's Frame of Reference*, Varkala: Narayana Gurukula, 1987.

———, *Vedānta Revalued and Restated*, Varkala: Narayana Gurukula, 1987.

———, *The Philosophy of a Guru*, Varkala: Narayana Gurukula, 1986.

Nitya Chaitanya Yati, *Neither This nor That But Aum*, Delhi: Vikas Publishing House, 1982.

———, *The Psychology of Darśanamālā*, Varkala: Narayana Gurukula, 1987.

———, *Bhagavad Gītā Swādhyāyam* (Malayalam) (Commentary on the *Bhagavad Gītā*), Varkala: Narayana Gurukula, 1989.

Panikkar, Raimundo, *The Vedic Experience*, Pondicherry: All India Books, 1977.

Prakasananda, Swami, *Sreemad Bhagavad Gītā* — Commentary (Malayalam), Trichur: Sri Ramakrishna Mutt, 1987.

Radhakrishnan, S. (tr.), *The Principal Upaniṣads*, London: George Allen and Unwin, 1953.

Rāmānujācārya, *The Vedānta Sūtras* — Commentary, tr. George Thibaut, Delhi: Motilal Banarsidass, 1984.

Raghavachar, S.S., *Vedārtha Saṁgraha*, Madras: Sri Ramakrishna Ashrama, 1978.

Śaṅkarācārya, *Vidānta Sūtras* — Commentary, tr. George Thibaut, Delhi: Motilal Banarsidass, 1973.

———, *Vivekacūḍāmaṇi*, tr. Swami Madhavananda, Calcutta: Advaita Ashram, 1970.

———, *Bṛhadāraṇyaka Upaniṣad* — Commentary, tr. Swami Madhavananda, Calcutta: Advaita Ashram, 1988.

———, *Chāndogya Upaniṣad* — Commentary, tr. Swami Gambhirananda, Calcutta: Advaita Ashram.

———, *Eight Upaniṣads* — Commentary, tr. Swami Gambhirananda, Calcutta: Advaita Ashram, 1986.

Śaṅkara, *Taittirīya Upaniṣad* (Hindi), Gorakhpur: Geeta Press.

Sharma, B.N.K., *Philosophy of Sri Madhvācārya*, Bombay: Bharatiya Vidya Bhavan, 1962.

Sinha, Jadunath, *Indian Psychology*, Delhi: Motilal Banarsidass, 1986.

Srinivasachari, P.N., *The Philosophy of Viśiṣṭādvaita*, Madras: Adayar Library, 1970.

Srinivasadasa, *Yatīndramata Dīpikā*, Madras: Sri Ramakrishna Math, 1978.

Sukumar Azhikode, *Tattvamasi* (Malayalam), Kottayam: National Book Stall, 1988.

Upaniṣad Saṁgrahaḥ, Delhi: Motilal Banarsidass, 1980.

Vidyananda Swami, *Darśanamāla* — Commentary (Malayalam), Varkala: Sivagiri Mutt, 1976.

Zukav, Gary, *The Dancing Wu Li Masters*, Glasgow: Fantana Paperbacks, 1989.

Index